BRISTOL

Edited by Allison Dowse

First published in Great Britain in 1999 by
POETRY NOW YOUNG WRITERS
Remus House,
Coltsfoot Drive,
Woodston,
Peterborough, PE2 9JX
Telephone (01733) 890066

HB ISBN 0 75431 502 9
SB ISBN 0 75431 503 7

FOREWORD

Poetry Now Young Writers have produced poetry books in conjunction with schools for over eight years; providing a platform for talented young people to shine. This year, the Celebration 2000 collection of regional anthologies were developed with the millennium in mind.

With the nation taking stock of how far we have come, and reflecting on what we want to achieve in the future, our anthologies give a vivid insight into the thoughts and experiences of the younger generation.

We were once again impressed with the quality and attention to detail of every entry received and hope you will enjoy the poems we have decided to feature in *Celebration 2000 Bristol* for many years to come.

CONTENTS

Hollie Godrich	88
Stuart Payne	89
Sarah-Leigh Osborn	90
Sebastian Pike	90
Martin Worgan	91
Lydia Clayphan Turner	91
Georgina Hooper	92
Gerald Burdett	92

Henbury Court Primary School

Jennifer Gray	93
Hayley James	93
Samantha Wootten	94
Lauren Graves	94
Ben Beecroft	95
Jonathan Verdon	95
Luke Boston	96
Helen Thomas	96
Robert Andrew Rees	97
Krystal Jarvis	97
Adam Cavill	98
Rebecca Hale	98
Daniel Nightingale	98
Kirstie Goodman	99
Kayleigh Hayward	99
Jamie Wall	99
Alice Thorn	100
Carly Cookson	100
Christopher Love	101
Edward Wright	101
Jack Cotter	102
Roxanne Edwards	102
Georgina Powell	103
Joel Bryant	103
Lucy Partridge	103
Karl F Whittaker	104

Sefton Park Junior School

Thomas Thurston	195
Florence Greenland-Hall	195
Lee Mitchell	196
Nyame Stranger	196
Joseph Johnstone	197
William Nixon	197
Rachael Milner-Lunt	198
Ashley Barnes	199
Karl-Johan Gasiorek	199
Samantha Coggins	199
Katerina Lockett	200
Samuel Varcoe	200
April Pearson	201
Stefan Williams	201

Summerhill Junior School

Leanne Roost	202
Amy Conaboy	202
Kerri Edgar	203
Chloe Allward	203
Jenny Frampton	204
Samuel Bracey	204

The Meadows Primary School

Oliver Holt	205
Stephanie Crosse	205
Thomas Cole	206
Hannah Webb	206
Holly Bryan	207
Daniel Watkins	207
Sara Grady	208
Calley Williams	209
Lauren Davies	209
Clare Pearce	210
Max Holder	210

The Poems

TOYS

Toys are nice, they're good to play with
My mum buys me lots I like to stay with
I have little ones and big ones too.
But that's all right I like them all
Some so small I can fit them in my shoe
I've got so many I don't know what to do?

Anita Kaur (7)

THE ZOO

Elephants, tigers and lions,
Face paints, wow, look at Brian's.
All kinds of funny looking birds,
Oh yes, when I said elephants, there are herds!
Lovely surroundings for a picnic,
No, no, don't eat it all yet Nick.

Sophie Moule (9)

SMELLY, STINKY FARM

Smelly, stinky farm,
I hate farms,
They upset the pigs.
You can't see the sky,
There's too many flies,
The pigs are the cleanest.
I am a pig,
I am the queen of pigs.

Ailsa Tippins (8)
Abbotswood Junior School

I AM A PEBBLE

I am in Egypt,
On a cold beach.
I am a pebble,
Soft and round.
Now I lie on the sea edge,
I get washed away by the sea.
So bye, bye for now!

Now I am back,
I will tell you some more,
I am a pebble,
And that is not all.
I am in sand now,
I slip about and bump into rocks,
And other pebbles.

I like your pebble,
Do you like me or yours?
I will tell you how I got flat,
Because I was bumped about
Against the other rocks
And pebbles.

Sam Gane (7)
Abbotswood Junior School

I AM ASLEEP AT NIGHT

I am asleep at night,
There is a noise,
What's that?
Is it the cat?
No!
So what is it?
Oh no! It's in mum's bed,
Mum!
Where are you,
I need you,
Where are you?
Oh no! They've gone.
Ah, there you are mum,
I heard a noise,
It sounded like a ghost.
Come and see,
OK.
Can you hear it?
Yes I can.
I thought you said
That you saw a ghost.
Mum! I did! I did.
Just get back to bed.

Martyn Emsley (7)
Abbotswood Junior School

DARKNESS IN THE FOREST

I am in the forest,
It is very dark,
The trees are rattling
Like a shaker.
I can see my shadow,
It is like a ghost,
Taking care of me.
Crash! Oh no! It's thunder,
I'd better go home.
Oh no! I can't find the way,
Is it the right turning,
Or is it the left one?
I am lost.
I guess the way to go,
It is the right way,
I run home.

Charlie Lacey (7)
Abbotswood Junior School

IN THE GARDEN

The sun is hot,
I can smell the sunflowers.
I feel like the flowers.
I can see the sunflowers in the garden.
The boy and girl smell the sunflowers.
The sunflowers smell beautiful.
The boy and the girl can see the sunflowers.
The boy is smelling the flowers.
The next night all the flowers are not good,
The boy and the girl go home.

Luke Jones (8)
Abbotswood Junior School

A PEBBLE

A little pebble is so playful,
I am black and soft brown with a crystal surface.
I can hear people playing and laughing.
The stars in sky look down at me.
The sea is crashing on me.
I like it when the sea is cold,
I can play with my friends and sit on top of them.
A little pebble is so beautiful,
I am black and soft brown with a crystal surface.
I have ripples of black wiggles.
I'm hot,
I need some water quickly.
Summer is fine,
It's hot, hot and people swim in the blue sea.
The sky is blue with clouds.
The winter is cold,
The sea is ice and it's green and blue,
The sky is dark.
The clouds in the sky are grey,
The beach is hard and cold when it is snowing.

Rebecca Searle (8)
Abbotswood Junior School

THE PEBBLE

I was a pebble,
I was a big pebble,
I was a gold pebble,
Smooth with patterns all over.
I was smooth from the sea,
But I turned into a boy,
In a flash of smoke.

Ryan Turnbull (8)
Abbotswood Junior School

I AM A PEBBLE

I am a pebble on a hot beach,
Another pebble is on top of me,
He is cold.
The sea pulls me into the water,
It feels like a bath
And it smells like salt.
In the sea I hear seabirds in the sky.
The sea teaches me to spin,
I can go down and up.
When I go down,
I hit the bottom of the sea.
A sea monster pulls me down,
And a sea fish pushes me out.
I arrive at Wales.
A wave throws me at a wall,
I smash into pieces.

Curtis Mears (7)
Abbotswood Junior School

IN THE MEADOW

I am in the meadow with beautiful yellow flowers,
I smell the lovely flowers,
I can see the dark blue sky,
I can hear the wind blow,
The wind sounds like whistles,
I feel like I want to stay there forever.
The meadow is very hot,
I run round the daisies, it is really fun,
The meadow is full of lovely daisies,
There is only me, the grass and the flowers,
I am going to sleep with the flowers.

Kelly Luke (7)
Abbotswood Junior School

LOVELY PEBBLE

I am a pebble,
I live on the sandy beach.
The sea washes over me every night,
I can smell the salt in the sea,
I am white and soft on the skin,
In one place I am bumpy.
I can see the sand,
I can feel people stepping on me.
At night,
In the sea,
I am as beautiful as a jewel,
At night-time I see the stars in the sky.

Lucy Davies (8)
Abbotswood Junior School

DARKNESS IN THE HOUSE

I was in my bed,
I was watching TV,
When my dad came up.
I switched my TV off,
And turned the light on.
He says 'Goodnight,'
He shuts the door.
It is silent,
And I go silent.
I close my eyes,
And go to sleep.

Daniel Gosling (7)
Abbotswood Junior School

Searching For A Great Tomb

Searching for a tomb.
I'm an investigator,
I am looking for a great tomb.
I am walking through a rainforest,
The leaves and broken trees make it dark.
I hear the scuttling of the monkeys through the trees.
The great tomb is in a mountain,
I have the right gear to go up the mountain,
But it is hot because it's summer.
I see a patch of light,
It's getting bigger.
I look through the light
And I see a gigantic cavern.
I look to the top and I see the great tomb inside it.
I see treasure!
I say 'I'll take it all.'
I walk out of the door
And run through the forest,
Hugging my treasure.

Adam Greenslade (7)
Abbotswood Junior School

Shining Flowers

The flowers are like the sun,
The sky is like a light.
There is a little breeze,
Like a little wave at the seaside.
I am a little sunflower,
I have a mane like a lion,
And a long neck like a giraffe.
My feet are in a warm grassy plain.

Ashley Evans (7)
Abbotswood Junior School

IN THE MEADOW

I am in the meadow,
With lovely daisies,
How peaceful and fun,
I wish I could stay here forever.
The blue in the sky is like a light in your eye,
And it's nice and hot and colourful too,
And we can roll,
In the meadow,
Forever by the sun.
I can hear birds singing in the trees,
And I can hear the sound of the wind.
It's blowing south.

Kelly Lane (7)
Abbotswood Junior School

FLOWER DAY

I am a flower,
I can see lots of things in my mind,
I can see the birds.
I feel sad because I left my home,
A long time ago.
I feel very happy because I have a birthday every day.
I have pink petals,
And I have a green dress to wear.
I live in a garden,
Where people live.

Emma Hembrow (7)
Abbotswood Junior School

THE GOLDEN EGG

I am a golden egg
And I sparkle too.
I would like to be alive,
But I am a golden egg.
If I was alive,
No!
That's impossible!
Because I am a golden egg.
I am shiny
And if a mum bird sees me
She will pretend to be my mummy.
I like how I am
And I am pleased with how I am too.

Once more,
I am a golden egg.

Jessica Sims
Abbotswood Junior School

NEW YORK

I am a statue.
It is a hot summer day
And the air is calm.
I can see the cars,
Rushing around.
I can see the skyscrapers
And people below running.
I can hear the birds in the light blue sky.
Here at the top,
It is hot.

Lee Moore
Abbotswood Junior School

LOOKING OUT OF MY WINDOW

Looking out of my window,
In the middle of the night,
I saw a scary shadow
And it gave me a fright.
It looked like a bear,
Tip-toeing on the grass,
It looked like a horrible monster staring all around.
It was black like ink.
I felt worried,
But it wasn't a bear
Or a monster,
It was my dad
Walking the dog.

Laura Gleed (7)
Abbotswood Junior School

A BABY STAR BEAR

A baby star bear,
In the sky,
Flashing like flaming fire.
It was sparkling so nicely,
It shone like hunters coming through the night,
They're sneaking on my pillow.
I looked out of the window,
Oh! What a sparkling, bright light!
I sit back in bed
And I saw
The baby star bear shining.

Shanna Patel (8)
Abbotswood Junior School

CRASHING WAVES

I am on the sandy beach.
I can hear seagulls in the sky,
I can feel my tummy rumbling,
I can see coconuts on trees,
It is like fire burning.
The trees are very spiky and green,
The sand is orange and yellow,
The sea is dark blue.
The waves are crashing on the beach.
I see a boat and jump in the boat,
The captain sails away.
The boat is red outside and in the inside it is brown,
There are five seats for four captains and one spare seat.
When I jump in and sail away I can see flowers and trees,
The grass is dark green.
When I get to the next beach I see a pebble,
I pick it up and put it in my pocket,
The pebble is smooth and grey,
It has got a red line on it.

Charlotte Swarbrick (7)
Abbotswood Junior School

SNOW

Sparkling snow, white snow,
Glistening snow.
In the night, snowflakes look like
Drops of white paint.
When the sun comes out,
Snow looks like
Little blobs of silver glitter pen.
When the birds come out
Their silver eggs look like snow.
The twigs on the trees
Look like white fingers.
The children make snowmen
That stand in your back garden.
'Where are your hat and gloves?' say their mums.
Snowballs fly through the air.
Bare trees, bare trees
Keep yourself warm.
Go sledging,
Go ice skating,
It is fun!
Wrap up warm or you will get a chill.
I like snow,
It makes me happy.

Hayley Wheeler (7)
Abbotswood Junior School

MY PET RABBITS

My pet rabbits are like soft pillows,
I lay my head on them,
They're so soft.
I put them in my garden,
They run like the wind.
They nibble at carrots,
They nibble at grass,
They nibble at potatoes,
They even nibble at apples.
They're grey like a rain cloud.
They run around in the rain,
And they get soaked.
They're very fluffy,
They get very muddy.
They climb up me,
Then I get muddy.
I put the rabbits in a run,
But they escape.
They run in the shed,
They always get tangled,
They hide in the plants,
Then I can't find them.
They're always so cute.
Sometimes cats come in,
They scare the rabbits,
But I scare the cats.
At the end of the day they jump in the hutch,
If they're good I give them chocolates.
I really love my pet rabbits.

Rachel Hales (8)
Abbotswood Junior School

THE MILLENNIUM

It's the night of the millennium,
All is quiet and still,
Like mice creeping,
Darkness leaping.
Then, the cat starts dancing
With the dog,
A person puts out a chocolate log.
A person blew a trumpet,
Everyone quickly gets out of bed.
It's the millennium!

After the millennium,
All is quiet and still.
Everyone thinks,
Wasn't it a special night tonight?
Children dream about the fun they had,
And happy years to come,
While grown-ups think
This is the best millennium of them all.
Royal courtiers dream
That the only better time would be a millennium
Where they could be
The King or Queen of England.

The Queen thinks
It was a lovely millennium tonight.
The bride and bridegroom think,
What a lovely night to be married.

Kate O'Leary (7)
Abbotswood Junior School

A PEBBLE

I am a pebble,
I live in the dark, dark sea.
In the daylight I am stripy,
Cubed and small, small.
I swim in the dark,
In the water.
With my friends,
I can walk around,
Some dark trees above me.

Jodie Batt (8)
Abbotswood Junior School

CATCH THE BUG

Every year we celebrate,
Have fun with the family,
Or with your mate.

Play music,
Learn a game,
Have a bottle of wine,
Over again.

Learn to skip,
Learn to dance,
Learn to jump,
Learn to prance.

You need to celebrate,
Have fun, be free,
'Cos the year two thousand
Is a year for you and me!!

Flora Sharpley (10)
Birdwell Primary School

2000

The year 2000 is drawing near and people
are starting to get in the mood for this year!

People dancing on big floats,
People laughing, dancing singing,
People having fun tonight as it's the biggest
night of the year!

I watch from my window, the fireworks going on,
They are red, blue and green, and the scenery down
below is the happiest I've seen!

The night is over, it's morning now and I can see
the sunrise as the last firework goes flying into
the morning sky.

Lauren Watkins (11)
Birdwell Primary School

CELEBRATION 2000

Year 2000 is here,
everyone cheer,
the biggest party ever
is near.

Champagne corks
popping in the sky,
as high as the fireworks
flying by.

Come and join in the fun,
and have a good time
because the year 2001
has just begun.

Zoe Fear (10)
Birdwell Primary School

THE MILLENNIUM BUG!

One week and counting,
RAM going wrong,
Sockets are burning,
Hot, hot, very hot,
Can't go on.

Four days till my doom,
Still hot,
Screen goes off,
Plugs keep burning,
Is my life worth living?
For I am just a computer,
Sitting in a corner,
A deep, dark corner,
In a young boy's bedroom.

One day to go,
As the hours skip by,
I want just one disk,
Just one floppy disk to save me,
For the Millennium Bug is evil,
And all computers should take care.

Bravo! My user has put in the floppy disk,
That one and only floppy disk that could save my life,
For the Millennium Bug is here,
So all computers beware,
While humanoids are partying,
We fear the presence of the Millennium Bug,
Who lurks in our processors,
And crawls in our memory,
And can never be forgotten.

Timothy Pearce (11)
Birdwell Primary School

THE MILLENNIUM

The new millennium,
Start of the next 1000 years.
Where will it take us?
No one knows.
The computer age rules,
But will it stay in control?
How will we travel?
Where will we live?
How will we look?
What will we eat?
Perhaps the start of less pollution,
No one knows.
We look to the future where the answers are,
The new millennium.

Sarah Webber (11)
Birdwell Primary School

MILLENNIUM

The year 2000 is nearly here,
Fun and laughter everywhere.
Fireworks, parties at 12 o'clock, till light,
Celebrating all throughout the night.

Will computers all shut down?
Will the aeroplanes hit the ground?
Will my mum's washing machine clean my clothes?
Will our video record my Simpson shows?
Who knows?
The year 2000.

John Deady (10)
Birdwell Primary School

Millennium Poem

The millennium is finally here,
Everybody give a great big cheer.
Lots of celebrations going on,
Robbie Williams even made up a song.
A new century has just begun,
New beginnings for everyone.
A Millennium Dome has been specially made,
Where things past and present are being displayed.
2000 years since Jesus was born,
Will there be a brand new dawn?
I hope that robots will help our mums
And they invent a machine to do our sums!
I hope that school will be more fun
And we will have more holidays in the sun.
I hope you have a Happy New Year,
Lots of fun but not too much beer!

Alice Alner (11)
Birdwell Primary School

Sonnet To A Snowflake

As I watch it
Floating from the skies above,
I see it
Open out its fragile dress
As it twists and turns,
Spins and whirls
On its way
To the whitening earth.

It has only a short time,
An instant to show off its transient beauty.
I gaze up in awe,
Wondering what it would be like
If I was a snowflake
Showing off my short but glorious life.

Katie Prevett (10)
Colston's Girls' School

NEW YORK CITY

The lights are on
in New York City,
It's buildings high
and tall. Central park looks
so pretty, people are always
so cool: eating American food,
hamburgers galore, lots of people
looking good in Macy's Department
Store. Ice hockey matches to go and see,
New York Knicks playing basketball;
tempting hot drinks like coffee and tea;
Empire State Building most famous of all.
Walk along Wall Street to visit a bank,
ride on the subway or take a trip in a cab.
See a show on Broadway, with famous
actors and film stars, or see a play at the theatre.
After a drink at the bar, shop in the great stores.
Bloomingdales, Tiffany's have room for us all,
up and down escalators visiting all the floors,
finishing our shopping trip in the food hall.
Home on the aeroplane with bags so full, I'll have
to call a taxi to help me carry it all!

Alice Myers (10)
Colston's Girls' School

VALENTINE'S DAY

V alentine's Day is
A very fine day.
L ove is important
E specially for couples.
N obody will be lonely
T onight
I f they understand each other and compromise.
N ight will be short
E specially on this day.
'

S un will shine throughout the next

D ay.
A happy love-life continues for couples throughout the
Y ears.

That's Valentine's Day.

Henaa Iayaz
Colston's Girls' School

PANCAKES!

Pancakes! Oh pancakes!
Pancakes taste beautiful and
Pancakes taste wonderful.
Pancakes are the best food in the world.

Pancakes taste delicious
Especially when sprinkled and
Sweetened with sugar,
Squeezed with fresh lemon.
Then pancakes taste luxurious,
Just the way I like them.

Why doesn't everyone worship them?
They must be mad
Those poor people
Who don't adore them.
They must be very upset and sad.

How could anyone resist them?
They don't know what they're missing!
When you fry them in a pan,
Spin them and
Toss them,
Then fill them and
Eat them!
Pancakes, oh pancakes
You're the best!

Gemma Leach (10)
Colston's Girls' School

MY CAT

He runs to the cupboard
When he wants to hide.
He chases all the birdies
When he goes outside.

He plays with my pencil
When I try to write.
He jumps on my bed
When I lie down at night.

He curls up like a ball
On the blue floor mat.
Thank you God
for my new cat!

Zoya Malik (11)
Colston's Girls' School

CHOCOLATES

C is for chocolate that I like to eat.
H is for happy which I am when I have it.
O is for orange as healthy as can be.
C is for Cadburys, Dairy Milk the best.
O is for Oreio the American chocolate.
L is for Lion Bar that roars all day long.
A is for Aero all frothy and nice.
T is for Taxi the biscuity bar.
E is for Easter egg the best in the world.
S is for Snickers as nutty as possible.

I love chocolate!

Camilla Godfrey (11)
Colston's Girls' School

I AM!

I am me and nothing other,
I'm not my sister or my brother.
I am ten and getting older,
Not so shy, a little bolder.
I am growing tall at last,
My days of being small are past.
I am happy, usually glad,
But when I'm poorly, I am sad.
I'm as hungry as can be,
When oh when is it time for tea?
I am tired, it's my bed time.
So now I think I must end this rhyme.

Bryony Wright (10)
Colston's Girls' School

THE BALLOON

As the burner ignites,
And the multicoloured balloon lights up,
It looks just like a light bulb
As we climb aboard.

The balloon soars up
Into the deep misty sky,
And the colours of the balloon
Melt into the sunlight.

As I look down onto the landscape,
I can see fields and houses like bricks,
People look like ants and buses like worms,
The streams are like ribbon: it's a patchwork quilt.

The balloon is floating on
But I don't fear falling out.
It feels great to be soaring through the sky,
Though my stomach twists and turns.

At last the balloon comes to land,
And it's very scary now,
As I watch the houses getting bigger,
And the basket thuds down and comes to a sudden halt.

Claire Price (10)
Colston's Girls' School

MONKEYS

Mandril,
monkeys live
on the ground,
On the floor
rolling round
and round.
Nothing stops
them from their
play.
Knowing they
need it every
day.
Eating lizards,
flowers and
fruit,
Yet fearful
always of
eagles that
stoop.
So through
the trees
they swing
a
n
d
s
w
o
o
p.

Jo Piddock (11)
Colston's Girls' School

STORMY TEMPER

Yesterday I woke,
Hearing the loud sound of music,
Made by the bad-tempered trumpets
As angry stones fell
From tall trees,
Like long needles thrown away.
I saw cars,
Being swept away by great big brooms
Descending a grey and angry sky.

Yesterday I walked outside,
To see fluffy clouds opening,
And white flakes floating down
To freeze my head,
Whilst a bright breeze patted me
Not so warmly on the cheek,
And a swirl of dust tore the trees.

Yesterday I watched,
White clouds open as heavy tears
Showered me with sadness
Like showers of cold water,
And drops of ice fell
Breaking rooftops
As if they were nothing
But beautiful wrapping paper.

But today the weather
Came shining through the window
With a message, loud and clear
Saying it was sorry about yesterday
And it was feeling more friendly now.

Iva Vrabtcheva (10)
Colston's Girls' School

GIGGLES

Where do giggles come from?
I wonder, yes I do.
Do they start from my tummy?
And are they runny like honey?
Do they hurry and scurry
Down tubes to my legs making them
Wobbly and gooey
Like eggs?
Do they simply go from elbows to knees
Making them go all buzzy like bees?
Do they pass my thigh,
Say Hi! And goodbye?

I think they go
From head to elbow,
To knees to toes,
But nobody knows.

Danielle Bryant (10)
Colston's Girls' School

WATER

Water falling then rising,
Then gushing,
Rolling and swirling.
Then still,
But still flowing.
Sometimes it trembles,
Then it might start bubbling.
Then it is still and quiet,
Just again.

Heidi Melford (10)
Coniston Junior School

GUILT

Guilt is a red blush,
It smells like dried up sweat.
Guilt tastes sour,
It sounds like a heart pounding.
Guilt feels like you don't want to be there,
It lives in you and me.

Chad Horseman
Coniston Junior School

HAPPINESS

Happiness is bright pink,
It smells like spring flowers,
Happiness tastes like sweet sugar,
It sounds like a running waterfall,
It feels like I'm sitting on some mountain grass,
Happiness lives in your heart.

Martice Hooper (10)
Coniston Junior School

FEAR

Fear is blue,
It smells like cold ice-cream,
It tastes like water,
It sounds like rubbing rocks together,
It feels icy and sharp,
It lives in the stomach of an iceberg.

Jade Rugman (10)
Coniston Junior School

DEATH

Death is black,
Death smells like burnt toast,
Death tastes sour,
Death sounds like someone falling from a cliff,
Death feels like a knife in your heart,
Death dies in your heart.

Timothy Green (10)
Coniston Junior School

HAPPINESS

Happiness is bright yellow,
It smells like pollen on a flower,
Happiness tastes like melted chocolate,
It sounds like soft singing,
It feels light and soft,
It lives in the good part of your heart.

Aiden Mitchell (10)
Coniston Junior School

DISAPPOINTMENT

Disappointment is purple,
It smells like poison,
It tastes like volcano lava,
It sounds like a fire engine siren,
It feels like the wind blowing across my face,
It lives deep at the bottom of the sea.

Francesca Redler (9)
Coniston Junior School

HOPE

Hope is red,
It smells like fresh air,
Hope tastes like an iced bun,
It sounds like soft singing,
It feels like silk,
Hope lives in your heart.

Lacey Flower (9)
Coniston Junior School

ANGER

Anger is red,
It smells like a hot burning fire,
It tastes like burnt toast,
It sounds like a roaring train,
It feels like sharp claws and sharp teeth,
It lives in a blazing building.

Kirsty Thomas (9)
Coniston Junior School

IN THE DARK

I've just woken up,
In the middle of the night.
It's as dark as a winding street,
As dark as a deep black hole,
As dark as the midnight sky,
And I feel scared!

Sarah Duddridge (11)
Coniston Junior School

THE RAIN

I can get people wet
and make people rush indoors
and make big puddles
and make people get out umbrellas
and make people shiver.
I can make big drops,
I can make birds wet
and make floods too.
I can be good and rain,
I can be bad and rain,
I can rain and rain.
When people put clothes out
I rain, people run in houses.
I can make grass wet,
I can rain all day,
I can go slow and fast.

Bobbie Webb (9)
Coniston Junior School

ONE ORANGE OCTOPUS

One orange octopus eating oranges,
Two tiny birds tweeting loudly,
Three trees growing tremendous leaves,
Four drunk drivers driving down the lane,
Five flabby fish flapping through the stream,
Six slippery slugs sliding on the path,
Seven men selling saxophones,
Eight men eating electric eels,
Nine nuns nibbling pastry in the nunnery,
Ten terrifying elephants tramping through the parade.

Max Biddle (7)
Coniston Junior School

THE SEASONS

Spring.
In the spring it is wet,
See how deep the puddles get.

Summer.
In the summer in the sun,
Down the beach I run.

Autumn.
In the autumn leaves fall,
In the forest foxes call.

Winter.
In the winter watch me go,
Making footprints in the snow.

Matthew Mann (7)
Coniston Junior School

THE RAIN

I can get people wet
and give people air.
I can make puddles
and get peoples umbrellas out
and make people shiver.
I can make drops
or make floods.
I can melt,
I can go slow,
I can go fast,
When people put clothes out I rain.

Callie Chard (9) & Shane Heal (8)
Coniston Junior School

SNOW

Soft snow falling,
Frosty trees,
Footprints in the snow,
Nice crunchy snow,
Giant still snowman,
Cold red cheeks,
Cold red ears,
The sparkling snowflakes.
Look out the window and look
at the snow.
Look out of the window and
look at the trees.
Not even one leaf on a tree,
The robins looking for food in the snow.

Samantha Pearce (7)
Coniston Junior School

IN THE DARK

I've just woken up,
In the middle of the night,
It's as dark as a chimney,
As dark as a cave,
As dark as my shadow,
And I feel scared.

Kerrie Jenkins (11)
Coniston Junior School

PE KIT

My PE kit's in the wash Sir,
It got splattered all in mud.
When my mother got it out Sir,
It then got soaked in blood.

My PE kit's all crumpled Sir,
It was worn last night in bed,
And when I got up this morning,
I found it in the shed.

Zoë Mathews (10)
Coniston Junior School

WATER

Water -
Gliding,
Gushing,
Surging,
Sea.

Water -
Tingling,
Trembling,
Bubbling,
Stream.

Water -
Rising,
Falling,
Splashing,
Fountain.

Water -
Meandering,
Swirling,
Surging,
River.

Hollie Coles (11)
Coniston Junior School

IF YOU WANT TO SEE A TIGER

If you want to see a tiger,
You must go down to the bottom of the jungle.

I know a tiger
Who's living down there -
He's big, he's brave, he's hungry . . .

Yes, if you really want to see a tiger,
You must go down to the bottom of the jungle.

Go down to the jungle and say,
'You big,
You brave,
You big hungry cat.'

And don't stick around,
Run for your life!
But be calm,
Be careful,
You never know where tigers go.

Leanne Ashford (9)
Coniston Junior School

THE SUN LADY

She beats heat down like a heart,
Slowly,
Quickly,
Then stop!
She quietly settles down to sleep,
She suddenly gets up early, ready to catch her prey.

Charlotte Dore (10)
Coniston Junior School

GHOSTS

The ghost went all crazy and went through the floor,
Wailing and moaning he sailed through the door.
He rattled his chains and set off the phones,
And proceeded to shake and pull out his bones.

Sammy Lippiatt (11)
Coniston Junior School

THE PHANTOM

Every night at twelve o'clock,
I hear a noise,
Among the hills,
Some misty black shape,
Following the night.
I can hear the noise,
It's coming nearer,
Thud, bang, whooooshhh,
Boom, boom, boom.
I hear a noise,
Gee up, ha ha ha,
I shiver, it gets louder,
Ha ha ha, thud, bang,
I hear a knock at the door.
I hear a whinny,
Then the clock struck one,
I heard a squeal,
I looked out the window,
Something flew away.
It went through the forest,
I waited for it to come out,
It didn't.

Amy Weeks (9)
Elmlea Junior School

WHAT IS A DAFFODIL?

A daffodil is a
Sign of spring as it sways in the sun.

It is a star,
Floating in the grass.

It is a yellow bell,
Ringing in the daylight.

It is a splash of paint,
On a green stalk.

It is a yellow sun,
Swaying in the long grass.

It is a lion,
Purring in the spring.

Alex Potts (8)
Elmlea Junior School

WHAT IS A DAFFODIL?

A daffodil is a star,
        Set right up in the night sky.
It is a trumpet,
        Blowing its soft horn.
It is a lion,
        Placed on a green stalk.
It is a splodge of yellow paint,
        Shining on the grass.
It is a sun,
        Flickering around in the sky.

Jack Davies (7)
Elmlea Junior School

WHAT IS A DAFFODIL

The daffodil is a big, bright star,
Hanging from the grass.

It is a small bell,
In the middle of the flower.

It is a splash of yellow paint,
On bright green paper.

It is a pen,
Drawing on green paper.

It is a gold flower,
In shiny green grass.

It is a yellow lion,
Hiding in the green grass waiting for its prey.

Jacob Goff (8)
Elmlea Junior School

WHAT IS A DAFFODIL?

The daffodil is a splash of paint on a green stalk in the ground.

It is a yellow ball on a blade of grass.

It is a yellow pen going to draw on a piece of paper.

It is a yellow bell at the church when people get married.

It is a yellow sign of spring,

It looks like a sun on the grass.

It is a flame on a candle on a table.

Ruby Jewell-Davies (7)
Elmlea Junior School

WHAT IS A DAFFODIL?

A daffodil is a splash of paint,
Upon a blade of green grass in the midst of spring.

A daffodil is a softly played trumpet,
Played by a soft turquoise stem in the brown spheres of soil.

A daffodil is a small star,
In the midst of night.

A daffodil is a lion's mane,
Being shaken upon the grass.

A daffodil is a church's bell,
Ringing upon the church's tower.

Joseph Lucas (8)
Elmlea Junior School

WHAT IS A DAFFODIL?

A daffodil is a ball,
With a stalk in the day.

A daffodil is an eye in the night,
Looking for the moon.

A daffodil is a splodge of yellow,
In the paintbox streaking across the paper.

A daffodil is a soft horn,
Played by fairies in the night sky.

A daffodil is a bucket of bees,
Searching for pollen.

Owen Atkinson (8)
Elmlea Junior School

THE DAFFODIL

The daffodil is a sign of cancer,
People wear it on their jumpers.

The daffodil is a star,
Floating on the earth
But there is not just one star, but lots.

The daffodil is a sign of spring,
As soon as I see the buds coming up,
I know it is spring.

The daffodil is a yellow floating candle,
Bobbing up and down in the water.

A daffodil is a yellow cat,
Walking on the soil.

Annabel Ballance (7)
Elmlea Junior School

WHAT IS A DAFFODIL?

The daffodil is a star,
Balanced on top of a piece of grass,
It is a trumpet,
Playing a soft country tune.
It is a pottery vase,
On a dusty table.
It is a sign,
Of springtime when flowers grow.
It is a yellow blob of
Paint standing on a stick.

Tim Rees (7)
Elmlea Junior School

WHAT IS A DAFFODIL?

What is a daffodil,
A bell that goes Ding! Dong!

It is a
Splash of bright yellow,
Painted on a white piece of paper.

It is a
Trumpet, blowing its horn proudly.

It is a
Sign of spring,
When it shoots out of the garden.

It is a
Glowing light,
In the middle of the night.

Keiran Marsden (8)
Elmlea Junior School

WHAT IS A DAFFODIL

The daffodil is a yellow bell,
Ringing across the light green sea.

It is a splash of yellow paint,
On a dark green piece of paper.

It is a bright yellow rattle,
Shaking green and long.

It is a long, curly fluff of silk,
On thin arms of dresses.

Rachel Hobday (7)
Elmlea Junior School

WHAT IS A DAFFODIL?

The daffodil is a sign of spring,
On a pale blue background.

It is a splash of yellow paint,
Floating in the sea.

It is a yellow ball,
On a blade of grass.

It is a streak of yellow,
Flashing in the street.

It is a yellow pen,
Gliding across the page.

It is a yellow bell ringing,
On the top of a church.

It is a yellow candle,
That brightens up the night.

Emily Fairbairn (7)
Elmlea Junior School

WHAT IS A DAFFODIL

The daffodil is a trumpet,
Waiting to be blown by the sweet-smelling air.
It is a lion with a mane,
Running around the garden.
It is a bell
At the church, chiming softly.
It is a star,
Floating in the air.

Oliver Clapp (8)
Elmlea Junior School

WHAT IS A DAFFODIL?

The daffodil is a splat of yellow,
Painted on a sea of blue.

The daffodil is a lion,
Roaring at a star.

The daffodil is a horn,
Blowing for the king.

The daffodil is a yellow butterfly,
Flying in the sky.

The daffodil is a flame,
Of a candle on my birthday cake.

Annalise Lewis (7)
Elmlea Junior School

WHAT IS A DAFFODIL

The daffodil is a yellow lemon,
Attached to a long blade of grass.
It is a splash of yellow paint,
Upon a strip of pale green paper.
It is a bright yellow star,
Attached to a pale green stem.
It is a lion's mane,
Attached to a long, pale green tube.
It is a bright brass bell,
Ringing in the church steeple.
It is a yellow horn,
Playing a happy springtime tune.

Mark Cohen (7)
Elmlea Junior School

THE WOOD

The trees stood high and motionless,
I could feel a shiver go down my spine,
The hairs on the back of my neck were
On end.
I turned,
High in a tree I saw a bit of red silk,
Hanging down.
I reached up and plucked it down,
I felt something on my hand.
I looked down,
There was liquid on my hand.
I was devastated,
Then I saw it!
A dark silhouette on the moonlit sky,
The trees were as dark as the night sky.

Thomas Sowerby (10)
Elmlea Junior School

WHAT IS A DAFFODIL?

The daffodil is a splodge of yellow paint,
On a green line of grass.
The daffodil is a star,
Hanging on a green line of grass.
The daffodil is a trumpet,
Blowing a tune of spring.
The daffodil is a bell,
Ringing in the church.
The daffodil is a yellow sun,
Kicked into the sky.

Reggie Reynolds (7)
Elmlea Junior School

A MYSTERY

Knock, knock,
The Listeners listened.
Who was at the door?
Silence, then
Creaking from upstairs.
Somebody or something,
Was trying to get in.
Is somebody in there?
They heard,
The Listeners went to the
Window,
Nothing.
But then there was a
Horse in the distance.
Was that him?

Sophie Shaw (9)
Elmlea Junior School

THE DAFFODIL

The daffodil is a green stalk with a trumpet,
Blowing its tune of spring.
It's a splash of yellow,
Painted on a sea of green.
It's a streak of yellow,
Charging across a field of green.
It's a lion lying down,
In a garden, going calmly to sleep.
It's a yellow star,
Twinkling in a dark blue sky at night.

Thomas Hargroves (8)
Elmlea Junior School

THE GHOST HORSE

Up along the hills,
Thud, thud, thud.
A misty, dull, grey shape,
Running along with the night,
As fast as the wind,
In and out of trees.
As the clock struck twelve o'clock,
It went away with the night.

I went out the next night,
But what I saw was scary and mysterious.
It was grey and white,
A whole herd,
Thud, thud, thudding,
It was like an earthquake.
And then it disappeared into the night.

Isobel Dawson (9)
Elmlea Junior School

WHAT IS A POPPY?

It is a red sun with a black dot in the sky.

It is red paint with a tube to hold it down.

It is a curled up spider in a dark red web.

It is red paint, with some days to go.

It is a red bell ringing all the time.

No one knows what it is, but I think it is one of these things.

Vicki Rose Harvey (7)
Elmlea Junior School

THE SILVER HORSE

She rides through the fields,
Day and night.
Where does she go?
When does she go?
She's like the moon.
Riding all over,
Never stopping,
How does she cope all alone?
Never eats, never sleeps,
Where did she come from?
How did she get here?
She's an athlete,
Running the marathon,
Ever going, ever longing,
Longing for something.
What is she longing for?

Clair Thomas (9)
Elmlea Junior School

WHAT IS A DAFFODIL?

It is yellow paint,
Dripping from someone's brush.

It is a lion, ready to pounce on a rabbit.

It is a shining star, way up in the sky.

It is a golden bell,
That rings when it's spring.

It is a yellow ball,
That kids can kick around.

Vicki Versaci (8)
Elmlea Junior School

THE PHANTOM ARMY

It was night. The night.
The night the Phantom Army came to be.
They came once a year, every year, until the end of time.

Part two

And they came, crashing through the forest,
Their leader in the lead.
They stormed past the houses,
And up onto the hill,
And then, they charged.
Crashing, bashing down the hill,
Down to their fate.

Part three.

And then, silence.
Next morning, all that is left is nothing.
The Phantom Army would do this
Every year until the end of time,
Unless the spell was broken.

Jack Holbrook (10)
Elmlea Junior School

SUN SETTING

The sun is setting on the sea.
The sun is orange as orange can be.
The sky is as red as a strawberry.
As it goes down in the evening, night wakes up.

Cameron Blackwell (7)
Elmlea Junior School

THAT NIGHT

One peaceful night,
There was a noise, it was a twig shattering.
It happened again,
Then I heard a bang,
Like a door being kicked down.
Then footsteps coming upstairs.
Suddenly he came,
Downstairs and out of the door.

Ben King (9)
Elmlea Junior School

THE CHEST

The door creaked open,
Into the house,
Spiders, sticky webs everywhere.
Rats scuttled about,
Faint cries of spirits in the cracks,
Up the creaking stairs,
Into the dark room,
Where bones glinted,
Everywhere.

Thomas Johnston (9)
Elmlea Junior School

THE LETHAL SCROLL

Once upon midnight's first hour,
A lonely messenger,
Wandering despondently hither and thither,
Trudging along with step, heavy,
Going, he knows not where.

This you see, many, many a cold
December's midnight hour.
No person knows where he met his fate,
All who followed are souls amidst the trees,
They met their end the same way.

Georgina Barker (10)
Elmlea Junior School

THE BLACK CAT

One dark night when I was
Asleep in my bed,
A figure rushed past my
Eye like a
Bullet on the floor
But to my amazement
I heard a snap and a
Crack it was just a
Black cat.

Milos Brkljac (9)
Elmlea Junior School

SNAP

Snap! The snap of the twig,
Echoing through the trees.
The creature chasing like a hungry mouse.
The instant fright of snap,
'Who's there?' he cried, scared.
Nothing but . . . snap!
It was dark, then a rustle,
Out comes a muffled sound.
'Are you a creature of the night?'

Robert Hughes (9)
Elmlea Junior School

THE MYSTERIOUS MYSTERY

Everyone in the village wondered,
'What is it that runs through the forest
And into our village at night?
What does it want?
What is it?'
One old man said he had seen it,
'It was white as snow,
With eyes that glistened in the moonlight.
You could just make out the shape,
Its eyes were pale blue.'
The man said he had seen it galloping,
Through the night, in the wind.
Do you know what it was?

Lydia Sheehan (10)
Elmlea Junior School

THE FOREST

I walked through the misty forest,
As the birds fluttered by.
As the wind whistled down my back,
The leaves dropping off the trees softly,
The rain sounds like a tiger purring,
Ready to pounce.
Suddenly,
Leaves rustling loudly,
The sound of feet getting nearer,
I try to scurry back.

Ben Main (10)
Elmlea Junior School

THE FEARS THAT HAUNTED ME

As I walked into this lonely, deserted house,
The door slammed behind me,
My heart pounding,
Like a lion roaring,
As I looked into the moonlit windows,
In this old deserted house,
As I cried out aloud,
'Is any one there?'
My voice echoed all around the airy house,
Phantom voices cried aloud as if they were trapped,
Books everywhere.
I never knew the fears that haunted me,
White gleaming bones all around,
Then as I went upstairs, I saw him.

George Gilbert (10)
Elmlea Junior School

THE TRAIN AT NINE O'CLOCK

It was Friday night and
Last night I saw a train.
It was a very old train but
Suddenly, I saw a camera.
It clicked,
And then it went on its way, but the
Next night it came back.
But then,
The next night again, click, click.
Someone was taking pictures of me,
But the click was like a flash of lightning.
Who was taking pictures of me?

Joshua Symons (10)
Elmlea Junior School

THE WRITER OF THIS POEM

The writer of this poem is as beautiful as a summer's day.
As intelligent as a professor.
As mad as a March hare.
As noble as a dog.
The writer of this poem is
As cool as a cucumber.
As kind as an angel.
As bright as a button.
As tall as a turnip.
As fast as a hare.
As stubborn as a stick.
The writer of this poem is
As free as a whale.
As tidy as a teacher.
As greedy as a grendel.
As cute as a cuddly toy.
As curious as a cat.

Harriet Lee (10)
Elmlea Junior School

THE STRANGER

A stranger,
Trudging slowly,
Up to the towering iron gates,
In the still silence of the night.
The stranger cries out,
'I am here.'
Still the silence carries on,
'I have come.'

But the moonlit mansion,
Still stands,
In the whispering silence,
Slowly fading,
From the lone traveller's eyes.

Sarah Gorin (9)
Elmlea Junior School

SAINT GEORGE SPEAKS

As I charged it saw me,
Black eyes filled with twisted evil,
Its teeth gleaming in the sun,
Fiery breath roaring,
As charcoal smoke filled the air.

The princess screamed as the
Dragon rose, its teeth gleaming,
I raised my shield in horror.

It shot a blast of fire, missing
Us by inches,
My horse backed up in fright.

Finally I got my wits about me,
My lance rose and I charged,
I hit him and got thrown off my horse.

I hit the ground with a thump.
The dragon was still,
I freed the princess and took her home.

James Wheale (10)
Elmlea Junior School

A Dark Night

One dark, spooky night,
I thought I heard someone or something,
Outside in the garden.
it was quite big and it looked rugged,
And it sounds like it has big feet.
I think its seen me hiding,
Where has it gone?
It has disappeared, oh well!
It was going to go anyway,
I wonder if it will come back?

Joanne Harrison (10)
Elmlea Junior School

The Wonderful Things About The Sun

The sun rising in the sky,
Burning high above the world,
The sun with beautiful colours,
Burning white, yellow and orange,
Flowers opening in the light,
Growing around the world.

Catherine Morgan (8)
Elmlea Junior School

My Senses

I see the flags waving 'goodbye'
I smell my mum cooking a pie
I taste the milk that the milkman delivered
I hear the cat miaowing purr, purr, purr
And I touch my lovely soft hamster

I see my granny coming to visit
I smell the candle that has just been lit
I taste the fruit that my mum has just bought
I hear a pig going snort, snort, snort
And I touch the soft furry cat.

Sophie Crawford (8)
Elmlea Junior School

THE SPELL AT WORK

The screams and cries sounded like hell,
The hideous tails of hair,
And it was obvious that the spell,
Had worked and had her,
As the screams,
Echoed,
Down to Camelot,
As he made his horse trot,
Up to the morning of,
The Lady of Shalott.

Carley Hogan (10)
Elmlea Junior School

WHAT IS A DAFFODIL?

A daffodil is a golden boat floating on a green sea.
It is a cream bell, ringing to wake up the animals.
It is a big, golden ball in the big green sky.
It is a lemon trumpet telling the sun it's spring.
It is a streak of lemon on a turquoise leaf.

Christopher Kaye (7)
Elmlea Junior School

St George Speaks

I went to England,
To fight the dragon,
I was a very good knight,
So I had to go to England.
But I dressed to kill,
In an iron suit,
Of the International Red Cross.

I got near the dragon,
And looked at him with fear,
And then I ran straight at him,
He tried to breathe fire at me,
And he was so ugly.
There was terrible puffing smoke,
That was like steaming fire.
He was green with nails
Sticking out of his back,
He was about four metres high.

I took my sword and
Hit him, between the ventral plates,
Then I knew he was dead.
I felt great.
Thanks to me. I defeated him.

Dee Hobden (10)
Elmlea Junior School

Unexpected Sounds

Unexpectedly a twig went snap!
He sprung round,
No one there,
Trees rustled in the breeze,
It was a night when the moon made shadows.

Snap! Another twig,
The man shivered in his old tweed jacket,
He looked around.
No one.

Anna Lucas (9)
Elmlea Junior School

St George Speaks

I went on holiday to England,
Because I was a knight,
They asked me to kill a dragon,
I put on my armour with a red cross on it,
And went to the lagoon.
I saw the princess tied on to a post,
And there I saw the dragon.

He was strong and mighty,
With wings on his back,
Which looked like the size of a holly leaf.
He was puffing smoke
And fire out of his mouth,
He had fangs and huge great ears,
He had massive legs, two on each side,
And spikes all down his back.

I had a lance and stuck it in him,
Just when he was about to eat the princess,
He fell to the ground with an almighty scream.

I untied the princess,
And took her back to the city.
There was a massive cheer.
The people all cried hip hip hooray.

Laura Carter (10)
Elmlea Junior School

The Forest

He walked through the wood,
He walked onwards towards the cave,
The full moon overhead.
Then he heard a noise behind him,
The snapping of a twig underfoot.
He called out 'Who's there?'
But there was only the sound of his breathing.
He walked on, nearer the cave,
Then he heard a sound again.
Yet again, he called out 'Who's there?'
But this time he couldn't even
Hear his own breathing.
He got to the cave, waiting for the morning.

Ben Tipton (10)
Elmlea Junior School

The Thing In The Swamp

I was camping in the woods by a swamp,
Unable to sleep, I got out of bed and explored.
Then I came to the swamp, there was
Something huge and brown.
But what was it?
It was walking into the swamp,
I decided to go back to bed.
I went to see in the morning,
Nothing there,
I felt scared,
I needed to find it,
But what was it?

George Devereux (10)
Elmlea Junior School

In The Middle Of The Night

In the middle of the night,
I went to a house,
The door was open,
I went in,
Then straight away I came out.
It was dark in there,
Well if you're there,
I did come,
I did,
I really did.
Then I rode home with my horse,
And said, 'I did come,
I did, I really did.'

Polly Garmston (9)
Elmlea Junior School

One Night

One night I walked to the window,
I could hear the floorboards creaking behind me.
Then I heard someone cry and cry and cry.
A black horse came trotting out of the woods,
The moon gleamed on his black shiny coat.
The next night I heard a strange howling sound,
Then a horse came out of the woods.
He was as white as the stars above him.
The next night I saw a grey horse,
I heard a scream.
The next night I did not see any horse,
So I went outside, and then it happened . . .

Ian Davey (10)
Elmlea Junior School

St George Speaks

As I galloped, lance in hand,
Confident of my aim to kill the beast,
I shouted when I saw her,
I rode up to meet her,
Man to monster.

She struggled to fly but her wings,
Were clipped,
She gave a weak spurt of fire,
But she knew already,
She would die.

My horse was on fire,
But that went out,
After a few seconds,
I shouted in triumph,
As my lance,
Plunged into the heart,
Of this unwelcome visitor.

I watched as she writhed,
Then turned, then lay still,
I rode home in triumph,
Proud of the work that I had done.

Vicky Armstrong (9)
Elmlea Junior School

My Senses

I see the children running to school
I smell the chlorine in the pool
I taste the jelly wobbling on the plate
I hear the children shouting because they're late
And I touch the rough skin of a rhino

I see the dog barking
I smell the good cooking
I taste the lovely ice-cream
I hear the sad boy scream
And I touch the smooth skin of the mouse.

Sam Rees (9)
Elmlea Junior School

ST GEORGE SPEAKS

I knew she ate children galore,
And terrorised people like mad,
She may have been pregnant,
But who wants more dragons,
The king of the dragons maybe, but not me.

I may be wrong, she may be mental,
She could be crazy or mad,
I'm glad her wings were clipped,
Or before long, there would be no Eiffel Tower.

Well anyway, nobody would want dragons to rule the world,
It would be really silly, for instance, Dragon Blair,
And King Dragon the First,
And the smell would be horrible.

The charities would be made, like the RSPCD*,
And the food would be disgusting,
And the streets would be littered with rubbish,
That's why I stabbed her between the ventral plates,
And stopped the dragon-kind.

(*Royal Society for the Prevention of Cruelty to Dragons)

William Fairbairn (10)
Elmlea Junior School

WHAT IS A DAFFODIL?

A daffodil is a vivid splash of lemon,
On a jade garden.

It is a golden flame flickering,
On a lime candle.

It is a star of gold,
Shining on the bright turquoise sky.

It is an amber bell,
Waking up the animals for spring.

It is a leaf-green bowl,
Of golden custard.

Oliver Singleton (8)
Elmlea Junior School

THE PONY

I looked out the window,
Once again, a pony galloped,
Like all nights.
It sparkled like stars.
Then one night something happened,
He jumped,
But then he disappeared,
Into the stars.
He came out.
The next night, he galloped into the stars,
But didn't come out.

Aimee Rudge (9)
Elmlea Junior School

THE WRITER OF THIS POEM

The person who writes this poem,
Is tall as a giraffe,
As keen as the subject of maths,
As beautiful as a new primrose.

As bold as a baby hedgehog,
As sharp as evil,
As strong as a lion's soul,
As tricky as a fast ant.

As smooth as a bear's hairs,
As cool as thunder,
As white as snow drops falling down,
As light as a close-up of the sun.

As black as burning fire,
As soft as a baby's bottom,
As cold as ice-cream on a cone,
The writer of this poem is me.

Sabrina Kaur (10)
Elmlea Junior School

GARDEN

Leaves brushing
bees buzzing
cats purring
birds cheeping
butterflies soaring
a cool breeze whispering through the trees
apples thudding to the ground.

Matthew Lodge (8)
Elmlea Junior School

THE MYSTERIOUS OLD HOUSE

Ding dong 'I've come' said the traveller,
But there was no answer.
He tried again, but still there was no reply.
He waited and waited, but no one came to the door.
The traveller wondered what was going on.
He started looking through the windows,
But still the traveller did not see any signs of life.
He saw a gap in the wall, big enough for him to go through.
He went up the stairs,
The stairs groaned and creaked.
He started looking in bedrooms and cupboards,
Then he opened a cupboard door and Miss Pearl
Was sitting in there, tied up.
The traveller untied her,
But it was too late, the stairs started to groan and creak,
Miss Pearl said 'It's here. It's coming.'
The traveller said 'What's coming?'
Then they saw something appear in the doorway,
'Help!'

Kirsty Wray (10)
Elmlea Junior School

WHAT IS A DAFFODIL?

A daffodil is an amber person,
Looking up at you with a smile.
It is a flame on a jade candlestick.
It is a sunny light in an emerald green bush.
It is a lemon star in a turquoise field.
It is a splash of gold and lime,
As we go past in the car.

Jennifer Falconer-Hall (7)
Elmlea Junior School

THE WRITER OF THIS POEM

The writer of this poem,
Is as handsome as can be,
His suit is white as an angel,
And he's cleverer than you might think.

As positive as porpoises,
As sharp as a shark's tooth,
As tricky as a tortoise,
As smooth as streamlined seals.

As bold as a bull,
As quick as quick can be,
As brainy as a brontosaurus,
As good as a golden ghost.

The writer of this poem,
Never fails to succeed,
He's the only one of his kind,
But that's only what I think!

Andrew Corbin (9)
Elmlea Junior School

SOUNDS IN THE HORSE BOX

A scraping of hooves
A crunching of hay
A bellow of agony
A frightening neigh
A slurp of water
A munch of oats
And a small clip clop from hooves.

Julia Debling (8)
Elmlea Junior School

WHEN THE LIGHTS GO OUT

So when you're tucked right in bed,
So many terrors from the dead,
Many fled, many dread,
So many terrors from the dead.
Oh how can my puny brain,
Count the horrors from the hall
Of fame, I feel the pain in my brain,
Mounting up with the pain.
I wish I had a viper,
One that glows so bright.
Every morning my mum
Says I'm dreaming.
Dreaming's what I do,
But I know, so do you, it's not true.

Arash Mojabi (10)
Elmlea Junior School

WHAT IS A DAFFODIL

A daffodil is a golden star playing a trumpet,
In an emerald sea.
It's a golden fountain pouring out golden water,
In a jade garden.
It's a sunny star, sunny as the sun in springtime,
In a lush, green field.
It's a golden bell as shiny as a mirror,
On a jade leaf.
It's an amber face smiling at me,
On a green body.

William Shaw (7)
Elmlea Junior School

WHAT IS A DAFFODIL?

A daffodil is a fairy's dancing frock,
Put clean on this morning,
For dancing in the jade grass.
It is a golden symbol of spring,
High above the emerald grass.
It is a golden shining star,
In the jade sky.
It is a golden bell,
Waking the Easter Bunny to tell her it's spring.
It is a golden coin lying
Among the emerald grass,
Waiting to be found.

Rebecca Knott (7)
Elmlea Junior School

WHAT IS A DAFFODIL?

A daffodil is a star of light,
On a turquoise sky.
The daffodil is a fountain,
Arising from the bronze earth.

It is a symbol
Of the coming summer.

It's a streak of gold,
On an emerald stone.
It's the bell of life,
Ringing for all to hear.

Guy Barwell (7)
Elmlea Junior School

WHAT IS A DAFFODIL?

A daffodil is a mass of blonde hair,
In a sea of green.

It is a golden trumpet blowing,
To tell us it's springtime.

It is a lime jelly with blobs of
Custard on it.

It is a field of jade with
Lemons in it on a hot, sunny day.

It is a sparkly star, blowing a
Trumpet in a sky of turquoise.

Joanna Betterton (8)
Elmlea Junior School

WHAT'S A DAFFODIL?

A daffodil is a coin,
        Floating in an ocean of green.

It is a symbol of spring,
        Waking from his hibernation.

It is a trumpet waking the animals from winter.

It's a floating flower,
        On top of a green cloud.

It looks like a golden face looking up to you,
        Happily, now spring has arrived.

Holly Tyler (8)
Elmlea Junior School

WHAT IS A DAFFODIL?

A daffodil is a golden fountain from the gods,
As a gift of water.

It is a sun that's been fished up
By the gods.

It is a flare blazing in a sea of green,
Warning spring is coming.

It is a trumpet, waking animals,
Saying 'It's spring, it's spring.'

It is a face blazing out like
Golden flames showing light.

Sam Banting (7)
Elmlea Junior School

WHAT IS A DAFFODIL?

A daffodil is a golden shooting star,
Looking down at you.

It is a star playing a golden trumpet,
From a different planet, higher than the moon.

It is a mass of golden hair,
On a smiling face.

It is a golden fountain on the top
Of a tall green tower.

It is a cream pillow with a dent in it,
Where your head has been lying.

Imogen Lloyd (7)
Elmlea Junior School

WHAT IS A DAFFODIL?

A daffodil is a golden trumpet,
Floating across a deep green sea.

It is an amber star,
Playing on a field of grass.

It is a golden bell,
Floating on a green leaf.

It is a yellow dress,
Lying down on a jade field.

It is a golden leaf,
Floating along a bed of emerald.

Omid Mojabi (7)
Elmlea Junior School

WHAT IS A DAFFODIL?

A daffodil is green jelly with
lemon custard blobs on it.

It is a splash of yellow when
I am going fast in the car.

It is a golden trumpet with
a streak of green behind it.

It is a soft and shiny ribbon
on a pale green dress.

It is a cream star with an emerald
sky behind it.

Sarah George (8)
Elmlea Junior School

WHAT IS A DAFFODIL?

A daffodil is a golden coin,
Growing on a jade bush.

It is an amber star blowing a trumpet,
On a green stick.

It is a field,
Covered with bright lemons.

It is a stream of green and yellow,
When you drive by.

It is a sun,
Floating on a lime sea.

Matthew Yeandel (8)
Elmlea Junior School

WHAT IS A DAFFODIL?

A daffodil is a face,
that pops up and looks at you.

It is a golden star,
that brightens you up.

It is a golden coin,
that drops from the sky.

It is a bright bell,
that rings over your head.

It is a sun,
that lights up like a flame.

Sarah Spalding (7)
Elmlea Junior School

WHAT IS A DAFFODIL?

A daffodil is a golden trumpet,
Making a sound to say,
That spring is here.

It is a lemon cut in half,
Squirting out like a fountain.

It is a star shining bright,
Like a lighthouse.

It is a coin of spring,
Glittering in the sun.

It is a yellow ball on a pencil,
In the breeze.

Aaron Hopewell (7)
Elmlea Junior School

WHAT IS A DAFFODIL?

A daffodil is a golden star
bobbing on a green stick.
It is an amber trumpet
on a splash of green sea.
It is an orange fountain
tied to a leaf.
It is a yellow bell
hung on a sea of lime.
It is a bright fire
hung on an emerald string.

Daniel Leach (8)
Elmlea Junior School

WHAT IS A DAFFODIL?

A daffodil is a yellow alarm clock
waking up the animals in spring

It is an amber blob of custard
on a sea of lime jelly

It is a gold star
shining over an emerald field

It is a fountain
sparkling over a sea of green

It is a face
smiling for it is spring.

Alice Kitcatt (8)
Elmlea Junior School

WHAT IS A DAFFODIL?

A daffodil is a lemon dress
dancing on a lime stage.

It is a golden lollipop
on a stick of green.

It is a flame spitting amber sparks
on a field of turquoise green.

It is a golden boat sailing across
the green sea.

It is an amber light dropped from
heaven on a bed of emerald green.

Shaun Ashbury (8)
Elmlea Junior School

WHAT IS A DAFFODIL?

A daffodil is a bow tied in a
fountain of turquoise.

It is a golden bell waking up the
symbol of spring.

It is a flame of fire shining to make
a beautiful sunrise.

It is an amber sign to make life
come back again.

It is a splash of gold when you pass by.

Thomas Leeming (7)
Elmlea Junior School

SOUNDS OUTSIDE

Crashing bridges
Weakening bridges
Breaking bridges

Motorbikes zooming
Cars roaring
Bustling of buses

Fluttering of a bird
Buzzing of a bee
Ssssing of a snake.

Tom James Dryden Elstob (8)
Elmlea Junior School

MY SENSES

I see the butterflies in the sky
I smell the sausages frying on the pan
I touch my friend
I taste the cake in the shop window
And I hear the clock going tick tock.

I see the rabbit in the park
I smell the big fat juicy cake which has just been baked
I touch the monkey in the zoo
I taste the turkey on Christmas Day
And I hear the children screaming and shouting around me.

Rebecca Acton (9)
Elmlea Junior School

MY SENSES

I see the dog jump over the log
I smell the pine not at all like a vine
I taste the pancake that's just been tossed
I hear the jet plane fly in the sky
And I touch a freezing ice cube.

I see the cloud floating by
I smell the fish not far away
I taste the rich syrup with a spoon
I hear the baby shout and cry
And I touch the fluffy teddy with his beady eyes.

Oliver Brady (9)
Elmlea Junior School

MY SENSES

I hear the mowing lawn
I see the newborn lamb
I smell the food in the hall
I taste the chocolate from my mum
And I touch my toy cat
I see my brother cry
I hear my mum yell 'Get up'
I taste my cream cracker
I smell my tea cooking
And I touch my teddy bear.

Rhianna Jones (9)
Elmlea Junior School

MY SENSES

I see people walking by
I hear people say hi!
I taste the ice-cream on the beach
I smell the juice from a peach
And I touch my bedclothes at night.

Danielle Arbrey (8)
Elmlea Junior School

MY SENSES

I see jets flying fast
I see the ships with their tall mast
I smell the flowers in the garden
I hear the birds singing with joy
I taste a Marmite sandwich that really makes my day
And I touch my teddy its warm and soft.

Dominic LeRoy (9)
Elmlea Junior School

MY SENSES

I see the sea like a shimmering blue sanctuary
I smell the yummy toast
I taste the taste of Tango that trickles down my throat
I hear the screeching of my mum's coat
And I touch the slithering snake that slivers on the coast.

I see the planes shooting by way up in the sky
I smell the perfume by my side on my mum's dressing table
I taste the jam that is sitting on my toast
I hear the toots and whistles as the train goes by
And I touch the red paint that is sticky on the wall.

Thomas Sweet (8)
Elmlea Junior School

MY SENSES

I hear the sheep, their accent is a baa
I see an orange furry Furby laugh
I taste the slippery pasta down my throat
I smell a chocolate cake being made
And I touch a slimy octopus

I hear a dog bark in the dog home
I see a monkey jumping from tree to tree
I taste an apple, it tastes like an apple pie
I smell a flower up above
And I touch sticky treacle.

Emma Davies (8)
Elmlea Junior School

MY SENSES

I see the eagle flying over the trees
I smell the honey being made by the bees
I taste the hot pasta on my plate
I hear the children screaming at my gate
And I touch the ice-cold snow on the ground

I see the food in the shop
I smell the soapy bubble that pops
I taste the pie that tastes like slate
I hear the children slamming their gates
And I touch the trees in a summer breeze.

Stuart Davey (8)
Elmlea Junior School

MY SENSES

I see fields all covered in green
I smell the roses in the spring
I taste the chocolate in the shop
I hear my sisters saying 'Look at mum's new top'
And I touch my pencil case all furry and soft.

I see my rabbits playing in their run
I smell the cookies that have just been done
I taste the big fat juicy bun
I hear the people start to cheer
And I touch the big bottle of beer.

Victoria Florey (9)
Elmlea Junior School

MY SENSES

I see the dolphins jumping in the sea
I smell the chips, fresh and ready to eat
I taste the curry, spicy and hot
I hear the big boy saying 'Get lost!'
And I touch the honey, very sticky!

I see Manchester United score a goal
I smell the car exhaust
I taste the Chinese takeaway
I hear the crowd shout with glee
And I touch the little pony.

Robert Fairbrother (8)
Elmlea Junior School

MY SENSES

I see the dolphins jumping up and down in the sea
I smell the fish being cooked in the fish shop
I taste the sizzling sausages in the pan
I hear my dad snoring away at night
And I touch the squirrel going by.

I see the leaves falling off the trees
I smell the house on fire
I taste the roast dinner on the table
I hear the birds tweeting in the bush
And I touch the baby lamb being born.

Gareth Nichols (9)
Elmlea Junior School

MY SENSES

I see the elephant in the zoo,
I hear the baby cry and coo,
I smell the fishy seafood,
I taste the treacle, a bit like goo,
And I touch the slimy slug.

I see the children, playing happily,
I hear the birds sing in their tree,
I smell the flowers in the mud,
I taste the sticky, chocolate fudge,
And I touch the fluffy cat.

Danielle Breach (9)
Elmlea Junior School

MY SENSES

I see the sea as a great big blue sheet,
I smell the old socks of the navy's fleet,
I taste the taste of chocolate cake,
I hear the bells of Christ's sake,
And I touch the slimy snail as it slopes through the grass.

I see the slithering snake slide along the grass,
I smell the chocolate melting in the mould,
I taste the jam in the jam sandwiches,
I hear party poppers at the party,
And I touch the toothless babies as they play along.

Jack Rothwell (8)
Elmlea Junior School

MY SENSES

I see the saucers hanging by the window,
I taste the icing which looks like snow,
I smell the bacon cooking in the pan,
I hear the roar of the great big van,
And I touch the soft skin of a newborn baby.

I see the monkey laughing cheekily,
I taste the rich chocolate which is sickly,
I smell the dog food,
I hear the man who's in a bad mood,
And I touch the rough stones on the fireplace.

Danielle Ball (9)
Elmlea Junior School

MY SENSES

I see the green grass in the meadows wet with dew
I taste the chicken stew
I smell the burgers on the barbecue
I hear the washing machine that is new
And I touch fluff on my teddy bear.

I hear the car horn
I see my baby sister being born
I taste the chocolate running down my throat
I smell my mum changing my brother's nappy
And I touch my soft cat.

Freya Morris (9)
Elmlea Junior School

MY SENSES

I see balloons in the sky,
I hear people say goodbye,
I smell the cooking in the room,
I taste the cheese like the moon,
And I touch the furry kittens with their mother.

I see the teacher eating dinner,
I hear the music from next door,
I taste the food but I want more,
I smell the perfume on my mum,
And I touch the silk hanging from the door.

Sophia Purdon (8)
Elmlea Junior School

MY SENSES

I smell the fresh smell from the baker's shop
I see my hamster playing in her ball
I hear my pop music on my CD tape player
I taste ice-cream and lollies from the ice-cream shop
And I touch a newborn gorilla.

I hear a newborn baby cry
I taste Indian curry from the Indian curry shop
I see all the animals at the zoo
I smell lemon on a pancake
And I touch a fluffy little cloud up in the sky.

Melissa Mitchell (9)
Elmlea Junior School

THE CREATURE

The lord of the sky,
Wings of fury in the air,
A heart of heat,
Like a flaming sun in space,
The symbol of Wales,
Its breath so warm,
A living oven,
A towering inferno,
Slain by knights,
Feared by maidens,
Heavy smoker,
Paws like blades,
Teeth of steel,
Powerful giant,
A burning rage.

Frank Jayne (11)
Hambrook Primary School

SPRING

Spring is when flowers peep
and grow in the gardens.
Spring is when mother animals
have babies.
Spring is when the sun shines bright
and sparkles over the meadows.
Spring is great, children play catch with a ball
and have a wonderful weekend.
Spring is when cats have kittens,
cows have calves, goats have kids,
chickens have chicks ready for Easter.

Leanne Shears (8)
Hambrook Primary School

A TYPICAL SCHOOL DAY

On the English coast today
We expect an earthquake to begin
Followed by a silent fog.

At break we are certain of
A sudden squall like a whistly wind.

In the maths area a dull sky
A storm starts brewing
Boom! Thunder strikes.

At lunch a gigantic heatwave
Starts followed by heavy hail.

Then in the science hills
A rusty fog settles over everything
Interrupted by a flash of lightning.

In art today we expect a sudden splash of rain
Followed by a colourful rainbow in the region.

Daniel Starr (11)
Hambrook Primary School

A GOOD MEAL

Bacon and eggs, a tasty breakfast they make,
Along with some bread of a quality bake.
Wash it down with some orange juice,
Maybe finish off with chocolate mousse.

I could have an Indian curry -
Better get some water in a hurry.
I might get Carbonara pasta,
At cooking that I'm not a master.

I like foods that are quite spicy,
But ice-cream can be a bit icy.
Nachos I like with tomato and cheese,
To a massive crunchy pizza I say 'Yes please!'

Michael Crotch-Harvey (11)
Hambrook Primary School

HOLIDAYS

Counting down the days
from weeks before,
whether going abroad
or camping on the moor.

Buy some new clothes
and suntan lotion,
this queue's taking ages,
is it in slow motion?

The day has now come
we're leaving now,
'Shut up' shouts dad,
'stop having a row.'

No more time for rows
I'm having such fun,
here in Spain
under the sun

Trouble is I'm coming home now
it's just not long enough!
Oh well, back to cold England
with my gloves and earmuffs.

Emma Rees (11)
Hambrook Primary School

SCHOOL

I can't help but think,
Why do we have school?
All we do is work, work, work,
There is no reason at all.

When it comes to maths,
We have to times and take
I really could have done,
With a long, long break.

We have to write with splodgy pens,
And grotty felt tips.
The boys threaten girls,
To a kiss on the lips.

I suppose there is a reason,
School is not that bad.
If school happened to go,
We'd all be really sad.

Emma Lerway (10)
Hambrook Primary School

MY BEDROOM

My bedroom is a pig sty
It really is a mess.
However much I try and try
It's never at its best.

T-shirts here and jumpers there
Socks flying everywhere.
Junk on the floor and junk on the bed
Oh no where is my fluffy ted?

Mum shouts up
 'It's your last chance.'
Oh no if mum takes a glance
She'll go nuts.

Hollie Godrich (11)
Hambrook Primary School

IT IS TIME FOR SCHOOL!

Oh what a trudge
My feet won't budge
Mum gives me a nudge
It's time for school

I wash my face
My hair's in place
We have a race
To get to school

We have a test
I'll try my best
Those girls are pests
When we're at school

I hear the bell
My teacher yells
I don't feel well!
Now I'm at school

The day is done
I've had some fun
Off home to mum
I've finished school.

Stuart Payne (10)
Hambrook Primary School

PREDATOR OF THE NIGHT

As it creeps through a maze of grass
It sees a herd of zebra pass
A lovely meal, it drooling, thinks
But I can't catch it
There's a hungry lynx.

It let out a roar
Ripped the ground with its claw
But its striped opponent lay still
It remained there, among the trees
Staring until,

It leapt out from its hiding place
Startling the lynx with its threatening face
Its stomach, it decided, it needed to fill
So it pounced on a zebra and returned home
With its kill.

Sarah-Leigh Osborn (10)
Hambrook Primary School

A BLUE FLASH

A blue flash is all you see,
A royal fisherman it's clear to be,
British woodland is its home,
A slight splash and it's gone,
Swift as an arrow in a forest glade,
In the river it makes its raid,
A jewel in a shady forest spot,
A lot more efficient than a fishing hook,
        Kingfisher.

Sebastian Pike (11)
Hambrook Primary School

IF I HAD WINGS

If I had wings
I would touch the top of Mount Everest
and take some ice back, and put it in the fridge.

If I had wings
I would taste the cheese of the moon
and eat it and save it.

If I had wings
I would listen to the moon turning around me
and have a ride on the whizzer.

If I had wings
I would gaze at the fish and chip shop
and get some chips to go with my cheese

If I had wings
I would smell pizza from Italy cooking
and take a slice with me.

Martin Worgan (10)
Hambrook Primary School

WRITING

Writing is such boring work,
It never has an end.
You do it all day long,
And it drives you round the bend.

Writing is not fun,
It never gets done.
It always makes me frown,
Writing gets me down.

Lydia Clayphan Turner (10)
Hambrook Primary School

LOST TIGER

Known throughout the world I'm told,
The tiger holds his name so strong.
So how come this almighty beast,
Is ground into some foolish yeast?
For ancient Chinese recipes,
To cure their pains and aching knees.

In years to come where will they be?
Without their funny remedies.
No more tigers, they're dead and gone,
But the pain we feel goes on and on.
Prevention is the key, you see,
Make this hocus-pocus cease!

Georgina Hooper (10)
Hambrook Primary School

IF I HAD WINGS

If I had wings I would touch the air
and I would touch the sun.
If I had wings I would taste the sky
and I would fly across my house.
If I had wings I would listen to the sea
and if I felt like it I would go swimming in the sea.
If I had wings I would gaze at the people
and I would fly around the world.
If I had wings I would smell the seashells
and I would run across the sand.

Gerald Burdett (9)
Hambrook Primary School

THE CROCODILE

Here comes the crocodile,
Gnashing his jaws.

Here comes the crocodile,
Slashing his claws.

Down, down, down the slimy river,
Crashing, slashing down he slithers.

Is it a log,
Or is it dead?
Is it the tail,
Or is it the head?

Oh no what a shock,
It's not a log,
It's a *croc!*

Jennifer Gray (10)
Henbury Court Primary School

THE BUTTERFLY

The butterfly, gold and silver
glides his way around.
He is very clever
he doesn't make a sound.
Sometimes yellow, pink or red
maybe blue or brown.
The butterfly, the butterfly
he's somewhere around the town.

Hayley James (11)
Henbury Court Primary School

SNOWFLAKES

Snowflakes fall,
down, down, down
onto the soft white gentle ground.

Snowflakes fall,
down, down, down,
onto my hot and gentle hand.

Snowflakes fall,
down, down, down,
as they melt all around.

Snowflakes fall,
down, down, down,
newborn animals all around.

Samantha Wootten (10)
Henbury Court Primary School

THE PIG

Please good farmer,
Give me a home!
Give me a place where
I can roam!

Please good farmer,
I'll do no harm!
I won't even wander
Round the farm!

Please!

Lauren Graves (10)
Henbury Court Primary School

WOW! THE SNAKE THAT LIVES IN THE DESERT

Deep in a desert
Lived a sand snake
It was cool under the sand
And that's where the sand snake lay.

I'm hungry, what's for breakfast?
The sand snake thought
So the sand snake poked his head out
Of the sand to see if anything was about.

Oh what a shame, nothing is about
No breakfast yet!
Thought the sand snake
I think I'll go and look for some.

The sand snake slithered across the sand
Hoping to find . . .
A juicy spider
That's my favourite breakfast.

Two spiders, one desert mouse
It was the best breakfast
I've ever had
Thought the sand snake.

Ben Beecroft (10)
Henbury Court Primary School

THE WATER VOLE

The water vole scampers through the grass
Long brown fur as long as my thumb
Big black eyes staring at you
His long flat tail thumping the soil.

Jonathan Verdon (11)
Henbury Court Primary School

SAMMY THE LIZARD

Sammy the lizard,
Lives in the desert,
Under the sand,
Where it's very quiet.

The desert is very hot,
But Sammy can stay cool,
By burrowing in the ground,
And laying in his hole.

Sammy sleeps during the day,
But travels around at night,
Where he catches up with all his friends,
And listens to their tales.

When the morning comes around,
Sammy returns to bed,
Another busy night ahead,
Better get some sleep.

Luke Boston (10)
Henbury Court Primary School

THE MONKEY

Gracefully, gliding,
brushing, brown as the soil,
the branches creaking in the jungle,
Tarzan would be proud,
if only he could see,
that little monkey swinging through
the trees, free!

Helen Thomas (10)
Henbury Court Primary School

BLIZZARD

I woke up one morning
To a brilliant white glow
I opened the curtains
To a world full of snow
I saw all the children
Playing in the street below
I got dressed quickly
And put on my nice warm clothes
The wind blows from the Arctic
And would freeze my nose!
The trees are heavy with snow
The branches bend with the weight
The ice shines in the sun
As I climb the slippery gate
Snowflakes drift to the ground
Like a small whirlwind
Don't skate on the ice please children
The ice is too thin!

Robert Andrew Rees (9)
Henbury Court Primary School

CHINCHILLA

Sharply darting in his cage,
bouncing like a frog,
in and out of his wooden box,
his tail like a squirrel's,
dark grey,
sleeps during the day,
awake at night.
Nocturnal he is.

Krystal Jarvis (10)
Henbury Court Primary School

THE BLACK SPIDER

The black spider.
Hiding.
Ready to kill, scampering round his web.
Collecting his food.
Shining in the summer sun.
Crawling faster than a centipede.

Adam Cavill (10)
Henbury Court Primary School

THE ELEPHANT

Stamping slowly through the undergrowth,
Comes the big, grey elephant,
Plodding,
Grey leathered skin,
Grey floppy ears,
I wish I could be him.

Rebecca Hale (10)
Henbury Court Primary School

SPIDER

Spider hides in its silky web
Waiting for its food
When it comes, he will creep
Over and roll it up in its silky
Web for later.

Daniel Nightingale (10)
Henbury Court Primary School

WHALE

Whale gliding
Through the sea like
A giant hand stroking the sand
Jumping like a giant slug
Squirting water
Through the air.

Kirstie Goodman (10)
Henbury Court Primary School

DOLPHIN

Dolphin gliding through the sea
Jumping like a kangaroo
Squirting water through the air
Crashing through the waves
Diving down deep
Talking to people he meets.

Kayleigh Hayward (10)
Henbury Court Primary School

A BUMBLEBEE

A flying creature,
a bee, a bumblebee.
Bees in the day and night,
buzzing wings like a fly.
Yellow and black, still
buzzing in the sky.

Jamie Wall (10)
Henbury Court Primary School

A SPIDER'S LIFE

Oh give me a corner
So I can spin my lovely web
Catch some flies for supper
And have a nice, warm bed.

Oh give me justice
Oh give me freedom
Say there's someone kind in life
To give me a spider kingdom.

On and on and on I go
Spiralling round and round
Spinning my web again, again
All the year round.

Alice Thorn (11)
Henbury Court Primary School

PIG

Quickly trotting through the mud
Slowly sinking deeper
A mud puddle is a proper treat
For a happy fellow
Sinking, sinking, sinking deeper
As he moves again
When suddenly out of the puddle
The plumpish animal jumps
Off he goes for a nice, long sleep.

Carly Cookson (10)
Henbury Court Primary School

DESERT EAGLE

The desert eagle dashing the rocks
Nearly crashing and chasing after a mouse
Quickly flying down and picks the mouse up
With his blood-dripping claws.

Feasting on his victory food
Gnashing at the poor mouse
Then came along vultures to see this feast
But the eagle pushed them away.

They thought 'Oh let's go'
And left him to his meal
He'd nearly finished when the vultures were back
And pushed the eagle off the cliff and had a feast.

Christopher Love (10)
Henbury Court Primary School

THE FOOTBALL MATCH

I went to a football match one day
to watch Bristol Rovers play.
Oh what a goal from Hollaway.
Things were doing okay
until the away team broke away
and got a goal past Jones.
What a shame.
But oh no, Rovers broke away
and got a goal past the away.

Edward Wright (10)
Henbury Court Primary School

The Sand Sneaker

When you're walking in the desert beware of the sand sneaker,
He's huge, he's grey, he smells like clay.
His teeth are as sharp as a knife,
If he bites you he'll take your life,
He's vicious, he's scary and ever so hairy.

He's got a hump like a camel,
Nobody knows if he's lizard or mammal,
He'll suck your brains out if he can,
Once he's got you in his clutches you're in trouble.

People have walked over him,
Then the sand sneaker has come out,
And then you know you're going to sink,
Then they haven't been seen again.

Go over the dunes of Agwan, that's if you find it,
Then pass mirage sands,
And then pass the dead camel pit,
Then it's time that you watch out!

Jack Cotter (9)
Henbury Court Primary School

The Crocodile Poem

Beware of the crocodiles
they give you a scare.
With swishing tail and eyes
that stare.
With teeth that rip and crush
and tear.
Beware of waters gloomy,
take care.

Roxanne Edwards (9)
Henbury Court Primary School

CROCODILE, CROCODILE

Crocodile, crocodile
You're so scary
Crocodile, crocodile
You're so slimy
Crocodile, crocodile
You're so scrawny
Crocodile, crocodile
You're so scaly
Crocodile, crocodile
You're so frightening
Crocodile, crocodile
You're back like lightning.

Georgina Powell (9)
Henbury Court Primary School

FLY

The fly is very fast
And moves with little, thin, snappy wings
And they make a buzzing noise
They are little black flies.

Joel Bryant (11)
Henbury Court Primary School

BUMBLEBEE

Bumblebee buzzing happily along,
Bumblebee happily buzzing a song,
Bumblebee smells pollen and lands on a leaf,
As the leaf bounces when bumblebee sleeps.

Lucy Partridge (11)
Henbury Court Primary School

DON'T GO NEAR THE HOUSE ON THE PIER

Don't go near the house on the pier,
If you fear it don't go near it,
That house on the pier.

Don't go near the house on the pier,
The fog isn't clear,
It is as misty as fear,
That old house on the pier.

Karl F Whittaker (10)
Henbury Court Primary School

FROM THE WINDOW

The moon is creeping, silently creeping,
Up to my window.
I'm thinking, silently thinking,
'Shall I sleep tonight?'
Or shall I just watch, silently watch,
The moon drifting by?

Ria Newport (11)
Henbury Court Primary School

SNAKE

Slither silently along you deadly snake
And make a young child's skin scream.
Your poison will work, I'm sure of it
And then slither silently back quickly.
Then find some prey and kill it flat dead
And wrap up warm for a winter's night.

Jessica Hodge (10)
Henbury Court Primary School

THE CROCODILE

The crocodile has big jaws
also has big claws.
He was very, very happy
and very, very snappy
His skin is so scaly
he has to wash it daily.

Robbie Green (9)
Henbury Court Primary School

WOODLAND ECHOES

In the semi-darkness
When the last chorus of squirrels' chattering has died away
I stumble my way
To the centre of the forest.
The night sets in
To be the darkest I have ever seen,
As black as an oil slick.
A breeze takes to the air.
Suddenly through the silence
A piercing sound,
Again and again, quieter and quieter,
My dimming candle lantern
Informed me of its vacancy
Down in a rocky crevice.
It was an owlet.

Isobel Booth (9)
Henleaze Junior School

MY SPECIAL PERSON

My special person is my cousin,
She is disabled,
She cannot speak,
But can laugh,
So if you smile at her,
She will smile back,
If you are laughing,
She will laugh with you,
She has to be fed differently,
She does not like it,
So I feel sorry for her,
I have a picture of her in my room,
It is in a frame,
And I look at it a lot,
She never cries,
And is really good,
It is really difficult for her,
She is either ten or eleven,
And has lovely hazel coloured hair,
She is called Sarah,
And I love her.

Clare Hollinghurst (10)
Henleaze Junior School

MIRROR, MIRROR

Mirror, mirror upon the wall,
You really are no use at all.
Your purpose I just cannot see,
Because I'm only four foot three.

Daisy Lovatt (11)
Henleaze Junior School

YOU'RE SPECIAL BECAUSE

You're special because the way you're always looking over me
From the clouds
And helping me in school and out of school
With problems
With friends and in our family.

I know you know that I can be a bit of a storyteller sometimes
But you have helped me
To tell the truth
By knowing my stories.

I feel you here
When I'm stuck
And when I know you're there
I feel safe.

Why did you have to go?
It's lonely on earth without you
I never even got to say
Goodbye.

Laura Thomas (9)
Henleaze Junior School

SWIMMING

Under water, splashing water
Having fun but swallowing water
Weaving down and touching the ground
Coming up and saying waw, waw, waw
Then the sad bit
Coming out and going home.

Gene Jozefowicz (9)
Henleaze Junior School

WOLF

The wolf has gleaming eyes that
gets you in a fright!
And fur colour grey,
soft for his own delight.
With paws so
delicate and easy to walk on
I think that it's like
having furry slippers on.
Nose so cold and made for sniffing
I think it would also help him for looking.
Humans pass by a long way away,
they have no idea wolf's looking their way.
But something stirs, is it a rabbit or deer?
An easier size which carries no fear.
Mouth dribbling ready to catch his prey
'Hurry up move out the way!'
Behaviour like the setting sun
and more until another day.

Rebecca Shipley (8)
Henleaze Junior School

'IT'

It was dull and dark,
Slithery and slimy.
With a dog like bark,
People thought 'cor' blimey.

The people it ate,
And where it lurked,
Made it late,
For work.

Alex Nicholls (11)
Henleaze Junior School

SPORTS DAY

Sports day here we come
As quick as lightning
My Lord that thing is dreadfully frightening.
Here comes Judy as sharp as a razor,
Here comes Simon as clear as crystal,
Here comes Jack he's as blind as a bat,
Here comes Martin as round as a barrel,
Here is Alex as fresh as a daisy,
He picked up the ball,
As light as a feather,
Oh my Lord,
Thank you Heather.

We won today
That counts forever.

David Cook (9)
Henleaze Junior School

THE MONSTER DOCTOR

I'm going to have my brain removed
Because the monster doctor said.
I haven't got the technology to keep a steady head.
He said he'll take it out and pickle it in a jar,
But then I say to this old man,
'How will I drive my car?'
He then replied with beady eyes,
'Don't worry about your car,
Because when your brain is on the shelf
You won't be going far.'

Jonathan Cross (10)
Henleaze Junior School

THE CAR JOURNEY

Peach, why are sunsets always peach, orange, red or pink?
Green, blue and purple would be more appropriate for my
       taste in colours.
Chunky bits of cauliflower and broccoli form different
       clouds in the sky.
I have no choice but to look up at the sky,
If I dare to look at the ground it's just a line of
       blurry mess.
The pain I suffer spins around in my head.
The way I feel I could be falling through the sky at
       one hundred miles per hour.
Gradually I am able to open my eyes,
At last I can focus properly with my vision.
I know it's hard but I must try to not look at the
       dreaded ground.
Suddenly my dad calls out, he shouts and says,
'Look, look at that beautiful little green, blue and purple
       flower in the ground!'
How could I resist not to look at the dreaded ground!
As you know they are my favourite colours on that
       little flower,
But now I have to go through the whole process again!

Mercedes Collins (11)
Henleaze Junior School

DUNCE

I always try my hardest,
I always do my best,
I just don't seem to be as clever
as the rest.

They always get it done,
They always get it right,
They always do the fun things,
And I just get a rewrite.

Jordan Paul (10)
Henleaze Junior School

TIGER TIGER IN THE NIGHT

Tiger tiger
in the night
with big green eyes flashing
clear and bright.

Tiger tiger
in the night
you fearsome creature
tall and right
you look kind but you wouldn't mind
gobbling up the rest of us.

Tiger tiger
your eyes that shine
your teeth
that are bigger and sharper than mine.

Tiger tiger
your eyes that shine
you look adorable like you were mine
but you wouldn't mind
gobbling up the rest of us.

Emily Daly (8)
Henleaze Junior School

THE CASTLE

Richard's castle what a place,
Lovely hills and great landscape,
Walking up and running down,
Wobbly topply falling around,
Grandma says 'Oh such a sound'
But I still go around and around,
We go back up run, run, run,
Quickly back down the sun has gone,
Inside boring waiting there,
Still as a nut brown hare,
Getting hotter as the day goes,
Helping grandpa in the loft,
Now I start to get lost,
Tea time, eat time,
Having sparklers, great time,
Time for bed,
Don't want this day to go,
Good night, have sweet, sweet dreams.

Sarah Bell (8)
Henleaze Junior School

THE HOUSE OF COMMONS

Last week there was a general election,
By gum there was a big selection,
John Major and Tony Blair!
They're the ones who should make it fair,
John Major at his desk all busy,
While Tony Blair gets in a tizzy,
Who shall we elect,
Who shall we choose,
How can we be sure they're not on the booze!

Rob Weaver (11)
Henleaze Junior School

THE DOLPHIN

The happy glinting shadow
Of a school of dolphins
Appeared in a mountain of spray
They were dancing
And prancing
Twisting and twirling
In the school
Of dolphins
All identical
One
Has snapped up a fish
Thanking the fisherman
As it goes rolling on
With a gleeful crafty laugh
After they have gone
All that is left
Is bubbling foam
Dying into
The blue sheet of sea.

Jenny Mason (8)
Henleaze Junior School

THE WORLD TODAY

In the world, there is bitter hate and bloodshed,
But under that, there is love and peace.
In the world, there are problems and pollution,
But under that, there are solutions,
In the world, there is famine,
But under that, is hope.
Hope for the future.

Amy Travers (11)
Henleaze Junior School

Her Funeral

A dim peaceful glow comes from the tall wax candles, the wax dripping
sadly into the metal candle holder.

Four tall men, dressed in black march slowly down the aisle,
a carved wooden coffin resting on their shoulders.

The vicar walks solemnly down the aisle in front of them, carrying a
golden cross which glints and shines.

Quiet whimpers echo hollowly in the dark church,
The vicar croaks, 'We all cared for her.'

Flowers lie in bunches on her coffin, and the vicar glances dejectedly at
it and sighs.

It's never nice when people die but at least you know they're at peace!

Florence McClelland (9)
Henleaze Junior School

The Stars

The stars flicker by night
before the morning sight.
Stars clear and near
flicker when you hear.
Waxing, waning the moon goes
shining on the roads.
Stars flicker by night.
The morning is bright,
they're waving like a little kite.

James Sandquest (8)
Henleaze Junior School

MONDAY MORNINGS

Monday mornings are so hard,
'Cause we have to cut card

Tuesday we have the fête,
I always go with my mate

On Wednesday the teacher makes a fuss,
Over a little piece of dust

Thursday comes the Mayor,
But he's late for the fair

Friday is the end of the week,
And we're on a high peak.

Matthew Quaife (8)
Henleaze Junior School

THE GAME

Football's such a fun fun game
I listen each week to hear my name.
They called my name out very loud
You should have heard the crowd.
The game has started, I kicked it high
Oh dear it's gone into the sky.
The crowd stand up
To see me play
But there I am being carried away.
Football's such a fun fun game
Now I'm off to hospital once again.

Aaron Powell (9)
Henleaze Junior School

AT THE SEASIDE AND OUT TO SEA

See the octopus sliding in the water,
Tentacles sucking in ready for slaughter,
The dolphin jumping up, down, up,
He's hunting fish for his sup!
Swarms of fish just like bees
Closely together just watch and see,
Jellyfish in the water slipping,
Nice and small but with that nasty nipping,
Help! Here is a shark coming along,
Singing a very deep, low song,
A crab on the rocks down there,
With a very frightening stare,
Round near the moss down below,
Can't you guess? I'm a starfish, hello,
You see that plaice with those huge, big fins?
Go on fisherman catch him for dins!
Oh look is that a mermaid over there?
No, don't be silly, I don't care,
Rock pools on the sandy shore,
And plenty of time for sunbathing galore!

Sarah Dickins (9)
Henleaze Junior School

WOLF

Eyes of fear, threat and of hunger or glare
teeth that gleam, glisten and tear
snow white fur soft and silky
fantastic howl could shatter glass
snout covered with blood like shiny brass
teeth bared it's not a smile or a grin
creeping through the wood never makes a din.

Lucy C Rowe (8)
Henleaze Junior School

THE CHEETAH

It moved swiftly through the grass
Its fur was shining like polished brass
Its spots were as dark as the midnight sky
A look of trickery in its eye.

It found its prey, a nimble deer.
Every sound the deer made came to its ear,
It pounced and scratched and the deer lay dead
With a gouge through its head.

The cheetah started on its meal
Its little cubs at its heel.
Then she put the cubs away,
That's enough hunting for today.

Nicola Buckner (10)
Henleaze Junior School

THE SALMON

Smoothly gliding up river diving
slow progress the salmon makes

10 out of 50 make it home
always in groups but never alone

Each salmon looks alike
two have just been eaten by a pike

Leaping up the Niagara Falls
up above a kingfisher lolls

Three are lost, destination only a flipper away
then they made it, the next day.

David Cutler (9)
Henleaze Junior School

I'VE FINISHED ALL MY WORK
(Dedicated to my mentor Mr Wordley)

I've finished all my work
And I don't know what to do! . . .

I guess I'll check it through
Like Mr Wordley tells us to . . .

And now I've finished that . . .

I've finished all my work,
And I don't know what to do! . . .

Maths or English, art or writing? . . .

Or something more *exciting!* . . .

Maths or English, art or writing -
What could be more exciting? . . .

For a thorough academic . . .
For whom extra team points are an epidemic!

I've finished all my work,
And I don't know what to do . . .

So I think I'll ask Mr Wordley . . .
For some more work to do! . . .

And that might even earn me
Some extra team points too! . . .

Lisa Maria Bennett (9)
Henleaze Junior School

A DAY AT SCHOOL

Arguing among some crisps
Bawling girl pretending to be a baby
Cutting out some characters
Digesting food
Embarrassed by a friend
Failed in an exam
Getting worked up
Hanging around with a friend
Ignored by a teacher
Jammed a finger in a door
Knocking on the headmaster's door
Leaking flask
Making a model
Noticing my worst enemy
Overflowing lunch box
Performing twice a week
Quarrelling with a friend
Raising money for the poor
Scaring year threes
Testing a kind of food
Untying a shoelace
Volunteering to break a pencil
Walking around the playground
eXciting Christmas play.
Yelling to make it clear
Zooming home
It's home time!

Sophie Stephens (8)
Henleaze Junior School

PANDA

Panda, panda, black and white,
Hiding in the dark, dark night.
Run, run, run away,
From the hunters in the day.

Eating, eating all day long,
To get very, very strong.
But when the hunters come to stay,
All the mothers die away.

Panda, panda, black and white,
Hiding in the dark, dark night.
Run, run, run away,
From the hunters in the day.

Oh! Poor panda, my heart will stop,
When you, panda start to flop.
But I shall stop this, I shall, I shall,
I shall make this solemn vow.

Panda, panda, black and white,
Hiding in the dark, dark night.
Run, run, run away,
From the hunters in the day.

So panda, eat on,
Look after thy baby, till I bang the gong.
And then, when evening draws near,
The hunters will kill you, bright and clear.

Laura Sudworth (9)
Henleaze Junior School

STEPPING STONES

Along the stepping stones I go,
Begging that I won't fall in,
Clapping every step I get right.
Dipping my hand in and out,
Eating my burger day and night.
Frightening the fish away,
Great! I'm getting there,
Holding my mummy's belt,
It's so cool going across.
Just as my mum calls out, 'Lunch,' 'Splah!'
Kicking the football up and down,
Licking my ice-lolly,
My hands freeze,
Nothing bothers me as I step across the stepping stones,
Oh no I'm going to frown,
Playing eye-spy when we're getting bored,
Quick! Look there's a giant fish,
'Rapping my scarf around my face.
'Splash,' I'm wet.
Tip-toe, tip-toe I go,
Under the bush is an unused space helmet,
Valleys are nice but not like stepping stones,
We love catching fish,
'Xcellent stepping stones are.
Yelling, yelling frightens the fish away,
Zoos are boring but stepping stones are great!

Emily Minchin (9)
Henleaze Junior School

A LIFE ON THE CRICKET PITCH

A amazed by the crowd.
B bowling someone out.
C cracking the stumps.
D driving the ball for a four.
E experiencing a new life.
F flattering your opponent.
G groaning at an injury.
H hearing the roar of the crowd.
I ignoring the umpire.
J journeying to the Ashes.
K killing off the Aussies.
L living at Lords.
M moaning at the umpire.
N naming the players from the commentary box.
O offending players and umpires.
P preparing for match.
Q quoting at interviews.
R rushing around in training.
S singing the National Anthem.
T training every week.
U underestimating the opponent.
V visiting new stadia.
W waiting for a catch.
X eXpecting easy fame.
Y yelling at the umpire.
Z zooming batsmen running miles every innings.

David Wilkinson (9)
Henleaze Junior School

HENLEAZE JUNIOR SCHOOL

Abolish that noise the teacher said
Banning yo-yo's
Calling people on the register
Doing PE
Eating school dinners
Facing the board
Gate's closed
Halting when the whistle blows
Ignoring people that put you off work
Jogging at PE
Kicking footballs at playtime
Laying models in class
Needing pen, friend gets you one
Objects thrown around the room
Painting pictures
Quitting clubs
Racing across the field
Singing songs in the hall
Tackling while playing footy
Underlining words
Vanishing pens and pencils and rulers
Watching Miss Patel at class
eXciting work that Miss Patel gives us
Yachting club is cool
Zero is the answer for 10-10.

Sophie Buchanan (9)
Henleaze Junior School

A DAY AT THE SEASIDE

A arguing at the beach
B bouncing a ball on the beach
C crawling on the beach
D diving in the sea
E eating on the beach
F fighting on the beach
G getting in the sea
H hurrying to the sand
I injuring yourself in the sea
J jumping at the beach
K kicking a football at the beach
L laughing on the beach
M munching on the beach
N nagging my brother
O obeying lifeguards orders
P playing on the beach
Q queuing for an ice-cream
R running on the beach
S sharing on the beach
T taking food to the beach
U using a spade at the beach
V vanishing on the beach
W waiting on the beach
X exactly in the sea
Y yo-yoing on the beach
Z zigzagging on the beach.

Oscar Davis (9)
Henleaze Junior School

THE PLAYGROUND

A Arguing, then we lose friends.
B Bullying other people.
C Crying for your mum.
D Driving people mad.
E Everybody bullies you.
F Friends helping you.
G Galloping pretending to be horses.
H Hanging about with friends.
I Inside people are eating their lunch.
J Jumping and dancing.
K Kicking a ball.
L Laughing and playing.
M Magic trick.
N Number sums.
O Obeying teacher's rules.
P Playing touch.
Q Queen games.
R Remembering friends.
S Skipping with friends.
T Tripping over my shoelace.
U Up and down the playground.
V Visiting the field.
W Winning a game.
X X-ray playing.
Y Yelling at the top of my voice.
Z Zoo game.

Josie Edbrooke (8)
Henleaze Junior School

MY HOLIDAY

Amazing times lay ahead
Bashed my toe against the pool
Carried on meeting friends,
Danced all night
Enjoyed my nights very much
Feeling happy, having fun,
Gasped as I saw the belly dancers
Hugged the waiters
Impressed with the apartment
Jumped into the pool with a splash
Keeping my money safe for presents I need to buy,
Loved every minute of it
Making sandcastles on the beach
Nothing to worry about, lucky me,
Opening suitcases full of clothes
Practising my diving
Quizzing my friends about their schools
Resting by the pool-side
Shining sun beating down
Testing foods, yum-yum,
Using sun cream it's a must
Visiting the Turkish baths
Wishing I could stay on my holiday
eXciting times I have had
Yelling with delight at my sister. Oh dear!
Zooming home where I belong.

Amy Callaghan (9)
Henleaze Junior School

A Day On The Sea

A Accompanied by an adult
B Believed that we won't sink
C Carried all the luggage to the boat
D Damaged, so we repair
E Edited our journey
F Fiddled with the rope
G Gained more power to move
H Handled the motor
I Ignored the fisherman's protest
J Jabbed a smooth rock
K Kept on sailing in the boat
L Lacked a good sailor but we will make it
M Made another ten yards
N Nailed ourselves to the sea for a couple of minutes
O Obeyed my dad to do something
P Packed for adventure
Q Quivered did the boat
R Rained and rained it tipped down
S Said 'We can do it'
T Tackled all the weather
U Understood my father
V Vanished in the distance
W Waited and we waited to reach the shore
X eXclaimed 'Why did we go?'
Y Yawned I did, it was late
Z Zoomed to the shore. We finished.

Richard Foale (9)
Henleaze Junior School

A Night In The Park

A As I walked home
B Black sky
C Cloudless night
D Deep shadows
E Everything still
F Frightening feeling in the air
G Guided by the moonlight
H Howling wind
I I see a ghost
J Just there
K Keep walking
L Lost him
M Must get home
N Now!
O Open the gates
P Panting hard
Q Quick footsteps
R Running homewards
S Shadows jumping
T Trees swaying
U Underfoot by moonlight
V Very frightened
W Want to get home
X eXhausted
Y Yearning for my bed
Z z z z z z z z z z z z z z z z z.

Matthew Stenner (9)
Henleaze Junior School

HAVE YOU EVEN GIVEN A THOUGHT?

Have you ever given a thought,
Of what might come in time?
Have you ever given a thought,
If people will talk in rhyme?
I wonder what I'll be,
When I'm all grown up.
I wonder if I'll make apple juice,
In a saucer and a cup.
If there's any bad things then,
Do I want to know?
Well the answer to this question is . . .
No!

Have you ever given a thought,
Of the truth of the past?
Did the Ice Age come first?
Or maybe it came last.
Was Robin Hood reality?
Or just some story?
Was it lovey-dovey?
Or was it really gory?
I really want to know what happened before now,
But what I really want to say is . . .
How?

Henry Ward (9)
Henleaze Junior School

PARTY TIME

Little brother's party, what a pain,
Thirteen 4 and 5 year olds, it will drive me insane.
In comes Joe clinging to his mum, 'I want to go home!'
Josh charges in and mum and dad groan.
Bossy Belinda bustles in, 'I've got new shoes they're shinier than
yours.'
As my brother shouts excitedly 'Let's spy on the girls!' He starts to
creep
And the rest of them follow him just like sheep.

The magician is turning a tube of pebbles into sweets,
'But *I've* seen this trick *before*' Josh bleats.
And though she smiles and says, 'Hush now little dear.'
Under her breath I'm sure she adds 'Or I'll make *you* disappear.'
Joe's all happy now, like a dog who's got a bone
But when he reaches for his sweet he pulls out a stone!
His face scrunches up like a paper bag and tears roll down his cheeks.

It's time for tea and they're all grabbing sausages on sticks,
They poke each other with them, prick, prick, prick!
Belinda's piling her plate so high there's no time to eat just yet.
Suddenly I hear Joe shout, 'Josh is all wet!'
'Josh has wet his pa-ants!' they yell as mum brings in the cake.
Belinda boasts, 'Mine was *much* bigger, it took *ages* to make.'
To try to shut her up we start to sing 'Happy Birthday to you.'

It's 5 to 5 when the doorbell rings
Mum flies to answer it, you'd think she had wings.
It's Joe's mum whose anxious face appears first,
Typical! He's having fun now and she could not have timed it worse.
Josh is not so happy, 'I want my party bag' he begins to whine.
'They're a bit small' says Belinda, 'Not as big as mine.'
When they've all gone my mum sighs and pats my brother's head.

'I'm sad it's over mum, are you?' I hear him ask,
I didn't hear what she said to him but it sounded like a gasp.

Ellie Woodward (9)
Henleaze Junior School

TIGER BRIGHT

Tiger white
And bright.
When your mother roars do you reply
'Honest mum I didn't lie.'
So when you're running wild,
Other mothers are talking and saying you're perfectly vile.

But oh, yellow eyed tiger hunting for the kill,
If you break something your mother will roar *'Pay the bill!'*
Your black stripes, daring eyes (yellow and round).
Your padding paws stamping against the ground.
Oh Tiger, your mother is so proud with your black stripes and white
skin,
Surely in a beauty contest you would win!

Levi Marie Jenkins (10)
Henleaze Junior School

FROST ON THE GRASS

Frost on the grass,
leaf and bush,
snow on the field,
ice on the stream.

Out of nowhere, a white
wind comes,
hail on the windows,
kettle drums.

Snow and fog blocking
hollow and holly,
along the valley the stream is frozen.
Thunder and lightning,
down trickles the rain,
no doubt about it
summer again.

Sarah Ellis (9)
Henleaze Junior School

THE TIGER

Tigers are nearly extinct
They haven't had time to be linked
So less tigers are made
And only a few are saved.
So go to your local zoo
And do what you've been meaning to do.
So show some respect
And make an effort
To help tigers survive
And let them stay alive.

Benjamin Melarickas (10)
Henleaze Junior School

SWINDON FARM

The cheeping birds perched high,
Swooping trees sway from side to side,
Trees tower above in tree caves,
The hurtling wind winds up branches,
The crooked stile leading into the
Meadow where the blotted cows stand.

Clucking hens tiptoe on pointed feet,
A basket of goat food over in the corner,
Pounding horses splash about,
The swishing stream trickles with small wrinkles,
Winding alongside the path,
A plank benched over the river,
Sheep closed behind an iron gate struggling free,
And that is the life at Swindon Farm.

Kathryn Pardoe (9)
Henleaze Junior School

HOMELESS

When I wake up in the dawn
I wonder what it would be like
To have no parents, my life torn
Freezing and homeless through the night.
I think of begging in the town
As cold as I could be
With people throwing money down
Not even looking at me.
But I am here in my warm bed
My brother gives a hiccup.
These things rushing through my head
But then I have to get up.

Jack Phillips (10)
Henleaze Junior School

FRIENDS

I have a friend who's kind and caring.
I have a friend who's good at sharing.

We play lots of games
never call each other names.

I have a friend who stands up for me.
I have a friend who is thoughtful.

She is always there
never goes anywhere.

I have a friend who makes me laugh.
I have a friend who's silly.

She is always nice to me
and I'm always nice to her.

PS: That's why we are friends.

Laura Swarbrick (9)
Henleaze Junior School

TEDDY MEMORIES

Once I saw a brave, thoughtful teddy bear,
and I saw his enormous belly,
that flopped down as he slept like a funky soft ted,
with funny fantasies.

Once I saw his big, green eyes as they starred at me,
as if he was crazy,
and very energetic like a gorilla.

Daniel Cox (9)
Henleaze Junior School

A Sailor's Lament

It is horrid being on 'The Matthew'
And I am going to tell you what happened
First Johnny came to set us free
I thought woo hoo! I am free
Until he took us to 'The Matthew' by heck
It is almost as worse as being on a wreck
Everyone is being sick everywhere
And someone was once sick in my hair
I have had scurvy many a time
Each one was as big as a lime
Me and me mates have had typhoid fever
The scurvy is as squishy as ever
And I won't even mention how we go to the loo
My mouth is zipped tight but Johnny should be sued
We are almost there now, you will be glad to know
But I was getting used to the sea, oh no!

Bliss Gallie (10)
Henleaze Junior School

Millennium Animals

After the millennium the lion will have a bigger mane,
The horse will fly,
The lizard will have a golden flame,
The monkey will never lie.

After the millennium the tortoise will have some new running legs,
The snake will lose his poisonous bite,
The ostrich will lay even larger eggs,
The glow-worm will have a brighter light.

Zoe Leddra (9)
Henleaze Junior School

MILLENNIUM

Coming up to the year 2000
We celebrate in our homes
We say goodbye to 1999
And hello to the Millennium Dome!

Two thousand years have gone by
We've done amazing things,
We've invented computers and TV, we've even learnt to fly!
What will the next 2000 bring?

Perhaps holidays on Venus or Mars?
Chimps teaching in the school
Or maybe supersonic robot powered cars
And instead of people aliens might rule!

Emily Durant (9)
Henleaze Junior School

THE MILLENNIUM

In the millennium,
People will be clever not dumb,
The rat will catch the cat,
The hog will catch the dog,
Houses will be made of glass,
And teachers will be taught by their class,
Cars will fly,
And dogs will try to stand on their head upside down,
Clothes will be made of gold,
And grown-ups will have to be told not to sit and play with their food,
Calculators will be even smaller,
And giraffes will be even taller,
The millennium is here!

Florrie Arnold (10)
Henleaze Junior School

THE MAGIC BOX

I will put in my box
a magical mysterious musical memories
a mummified cat whose ears stick out and a
magical bracelet that would guide me all the way.

I will put in my box
a slithery, slothery, squishy slug, an
elephant with no nose and a witch in a car,
a gold piece of paper and the goddess Ra.

I will put in my box
a perfect, pecky, piper, pepper, picky parrot,
a dog with a bad tummy ache, a
cowboy on a lion.

I will put in my box
a piece of a person's brain, a giant with one eye,
a girl with no ears and a bull rider on a leopard.

I will put in my box
a flying, flapping, flowing, flattening footballer, a tree growing
potatoes and flying, fairy godmother and a wall made out of bananas.

Sara Evans (9)
Henleaze Junior School

MY FRIEND

My friend is someone who can stand by my side,
My friend is someone who is friendly and kind.
My friend is someone who I can trust and like,
My friend is someone who can make things right.
My friend is someone who lights a million faces,
My friend is someone who goes with me from place to place.

Kate Sherlock (11)
Henleaze Junior School

IN THE BOX UNDER MY BED

I will put in my box
The eminent words of Martin Luther King,
the unknown galaxies,
and the eclipse of the sun.

I will put in my box
The music of a band called Offspring,
lightning's ragged line,
and a nightmare in day.

I will put in my box
When England defeated South Africa,
a night I'll never forget,
and the moon being eaten by a mouse.

I will put in my box
Elvis' last moments,
feet fishing for fish
and scorching summer suns.

My box is fashioned from the alphabet
and numbers,
with armies fighting for other countries,
and money coming out the corners.
I shall drift on calm water,
and sunbathe on bright yellow sand,
and listen to the noises around me.

Euan Strachan (10)
Henleaze Junior School

REMEMBER

Remember the Beetles,
Michael Jackson and Abba.
It's all gone!

Remember bubble cars,
Mondeos and 4 x 4s.
It's all gone!

Remember shops,
Towns and buses.
It's all gone!

Remember Segas,
PlayStations and PCs.
It's all gone!

Remember John Major,
And Bill Clinton.
It's all gone!

Remember planes,
cars and jets.
It's all gone!

Remember blackboards,
rulers and rubbers.
Millennium is here!

Jonnie Notton (9)
Henleaze Junior School

WATERFALLS, TOMBS AND OCEANS

A swishing, splashy, windy, wonderful waterfall,
A mysterious, musical, magical man
And a dangerous, dumb, dalmatian dog.

My furry, cuddly, squashy panda,
Tutankhaman in his tomb in Egypt,
A polar bear at the South Pole.

A robber chasing a policeman,
Osiris with his death mask,
A ferry going across the deep blue ocean.

Man. Utd. winning the Premiership,
Loads of sweets and chocolates.

The fastest thing in the world,
Me surfing on a surf board in my suite,
Khepri on a jumping kangaroo.

A lion doing karate,
Me drinking 7up with friends,
All my friends playing football,
Me and my best friend Phil.

Alexander Coates (10)
Henleaze Junior School

THE LAMENT OF A GUINEA PIG

We shared our nest,
We gave each other food,
Then we would go to rest,
Even though I was in a mood.

She looked so pretty,
She was so sweet in her sleep,
She wasn't very witty,
Her alarm clock went beep.

I feel so sad,
I still have a friendship ring,
She never felt bad,
When a bumblebee gave her a sting.

I think that she is in the sky,
I think that she is the moon and stars,
She never ever, ever lied,
She could be now Earth or Mars!

Harriet Culver (10)
Henleaze Junior School

SCHOOL

English and maths
Learned in the morning
Some find it fun
Some find it boring
Dinner play at last
Out under the sun
It is so
Exquisitely fun
The whistle blows
Everyone in
Dinner in tummy
Wrappers in bin
Back in the class
Science again
Jane lost her ruler
I lost my pen
Bell chimes for home time
Hip hip hooray
That is the tale of a
Normal school day.

Charlotte Mei-Ying Jones (9)
Henleaze Junior School

THE MAGIC BOX

I will put in my box

A shark which is afraid of sheep,
an alligator with no teeth
and a baby who scored a hat trick against
Peter Schmeichel.

I will put in my box

A mouse with horns and a terrifying face,
a mother sucking up dirt with a broom
and a witch riding a vacuum cleaner.

I will put in my box

A vampire bat running in athletics
and a man sucking people's blood.

I will put in my box

A wishing ring from a wizard,
the Everton football team
and a miniature size universe.

My box is fashioned from bronze,
fire and iron with bubbles on the lid
and secrets in the corners,
its hinges are made from dry clay.

I shall surf in my box
with a professional scuba diver
pulling me along the way.

Jack McKenna (9)
Henleaze Junior School

FEELING WORRIED

Once, on a Monday morning,
I realised I'd forgotten my reading book.
Then I realised I'd lost it,
When I went home to have a look.

I decided not to tell the teacher,
For she might not find out about it.
But with so many things on my mind,
I could have gone without it!

I could not forget about it,
I had nightmares about it in bed.
Also it was causing a headache,
Throbbing through my head.

For a split second I changed my mind,
Because my teacher might not be cross.
I kept telling myself that a reading book,
Probably wasn't a big loss.

I decided, in the end,
My teacher should know.
But my progress in telling her
Was very slow.

So as I just said,
I didn't tell her in a hurry.
But as it turned out,
I need not have worried!

My teacher was not cross,
She just helped me find it.
She searched my drawer,
And found the book . . . behind it!

Emma Watson (8)
Henleaze Junior School

Bubble Memories

I love blowing bubbles then watching them float away.

Once I blew a bubble that was as big as me, it was so big
that it absorbed me inside.

I floated upwards in my bubble up to the sky, my bubble went
even further upwards and silently stopped in the heavens.

The heavens were beautiful and dreamy and twinkling like glitter,
this was the most marvellous place in the world.

It was such a relaxed place glittering all the time, sparkling like
a crystal hall in all its glory and pride.

As I said before it was dreamy and soon I was fast asleep.

When I woke up my bubble was gone and I was lying in my
warm cosy bed.

Elaine Andrew (10)
Henleaze Junior School

A Boy With A Chance

The computer was broke and so was the school,
So I went to a club with a shirt and a ball.
I said to the manager, 'Will you pay me
To play in your team and score goals like a dream?'
The manager said, 'Go on have a go,'
I scored loads of goals, oh what a show.
I went back to school with 1,000 pounds,
Then they were saying 'There's Owen in town.'
And then I was famous, a millionaire too,
But I went back to school for a dance at the do.

Henry Dickinson (11)
Henleaze Junior School

THE MILLENNIUM MOUSE

Hi I'm the millennium mouse,
I live in a super cheese house,
My drink is barley pop,
And I like it with noodles on top.

I am rainbow with black polka dots,
And I never get any spots,
A robot as my maid,
Soon everyone will use them,
Maybe even in Big Ben.

If you never can find a good meal,
Then try Mars or Milky Way for good deals,
If you want to see the eclipse,
Then go for rides in spaceships.

It's the Millennium Dome,
Soon it will be your home,
If you have a magic eye,
See me say 'Bye bye.'

Jo Whittet (9)
Henleaze Junior School

THE OLD AND THE NEW YEAR

The old year has gone and the new year has come,
We forget about old hopes and fears.

The new year is like a blank sheet of paper
To be filled with new hopes and fears.

New buds open, animals take their first breath.
It's all like an adventure waiting to be done.

David Walker (11)
Henleaze Junior School

THE WOODS

As the day breaks,
The wood awakens,
Squirrels scurry from tree to tree,
Sly foxes creep in the brightening light,
Leaves rustle and crumple in the gentle tossing wind,
High branches sway like seaweed in the tide.

As dusk draws closer,
The sun sinks,
Owls as silent as night swoop for their prey,
Bats emerge from caves circling and diving,
Fog drops and dew litters the grass,
The cold of the night hovers over the ghostly woods.

Jeff Andrews (11)
Henleaze Junior School

THE TIGER

Camouflaged in the undergrowth,
The tiger studied his prey,
He focused on it carefully
It was to feed him for that day.
The tiger gave a hungry growl,
The antelope's ears pricked up,
The tiger crouched,
The tiger pounced,
The tiger ran,
But the quick witted antelope got away.
Enraged,
The tiger slunk back into the shrubs.

Clare Orchard (11)
Henleaze Junior School

MILLENNIUM JOURNEY

The path of yesteryears fades away,
The new esplanade appears,
Who knows where this track will take me,
Into the next thousand years.

Untouched, no footsteps on the trail,
No signposts to guide the way,
Plodding on as the months pass,
On the boulevard night and day.

Wandering along the avenue,
Of fun, of grief, of fears,
Who knows where this track will take me,
Into the next thousand years.

Katherine Hooper (11)
Henleaze Junior School

THE GRAVEYARD

The moonlight shone on the church graveyard,
Showing the names of the dead.
There wasn't a sound to be heard,
Except the creaking of the gate.
It was no wonder that nobody dared to pass it,
Then suddenly there was a movement.
A wisp of transparent smoke rose up from the ground,
It floated through the gates, and disappeared.
The ghost flew around the deserted city,
But as the day grew nearer,
the ghost returned to its grave.
And it's as if nothing had ever happened.

Hannah Swarbrick (11)
Henleaze Junior School

The Giant, The Farmer And His Son, Tom

It happened on a chilly, dark, winter's morn,
When the farmer's son was collecting the corn.
He heard a rustle nearby his house,
And didn't look up because he thought it was a mouse.
Later on in the day,
The farmer was stacking the hay.
He looked up expecting to see his working son,
But instead he saw none.
In front of him was a giant so tall,
You couldn't see his head at all.
The farmer had a real fright.
His face was turning completely white.
The monster called down, 'I've got your son.
I'll show you where he is, so come.'
Meanwhile the son had escaped,
While the farmer just watched and gaped.
In the end the farmer and his son got together,
And hid from the giant in some heather.
I don't know what happened before that,
I was told this story by Uncle Matt!
The giant gave up looking for the farmer and Tom,
And went back to where he had originally come from.
The farmer and Tom went away on a train,
And the giant never came back again.

Emily Browne (11)
Henleaze Junior School

Mums

Mums are great,
Mums are cool,
Mums are the best thing of all,
Mums help out with this and that,
They love having a chat, chat, chat!

Mums work wonders,
Mums work charms,
They know when you're being harmed,
Mums take care of the cat and you,
They always know just what to do.

Fiona Rugg (11)
Henleaze Junior School

MY SISTER

My sister is special because
She always plays with me.
She took me out on my birthday
And brought me lots of presents.
She's special because
When she visited my gran
She took me as well.
She's special because
When I was little
She and her friend
Did me and my sister a show.
She never complains
Even if I'm nasty
And she never gets cross.
When she's working in her room,
She always lets me come in
And talk to her.
She's special because
When we went on holiday
She let me share a room with her.
I wish she could stay
But she's leaving next year.

Laura Dimond (10)
Henleaze Junior School

SNEAKY FOX

Sleek, rusty and swift,
As sly as a fox.
His ears pricked,
He darted for cover.

Sneaking through the long weaken grass,
His eyes grow big clear as glass.
They're bold as marbles, brown as chocolate,
With his eyes he's spying for his prey.

He hears it getting closer and closer,
But the prey does not know the fox is waiting.
They see each other, and stop,
Staring at each other for a split second.

His prey has gone, he is alone,
He scampered back through the weaken grass.
Still hungry and curled up for an afternoon nap.

Natasha Reygate (11)
Henleaze Junior School

WHEN I WAS LONELY

Once, I went into the playground,
I asked if I could play with them!
In one big voice they shouted 'No!'
I sat down on a bench,
A tear trickled down my face,
Then another, then another.
They didn't play with me
For two whole days,
Then finally I asked them once again
And I played until I could play no more.

Jamie Hughes (7)
Henleaze Junior School

GRANDPA'S HOUSE

The windy stair like a
Lighthouse
A tiny cottage
All cosy and warm
Crackling fire flames
Dodging about
The land nearly all flat
No bumps or hills though
Blowing winds whistling
Through the trees
Beside the seaside
The sea is swishing
And sloshing
I hop from rock to rock
I worship the seaside
The seaweed all bouncy and
Wet
At night it is as black as
Coal
And the stars twinkling gently.

Hilary Orchard (9)
Henleaze Junior School

OUR FIGHT WILL NEVER END

F ights are common with my friends.
R otten we all are, and I don't like it.
I have to admit it is me as well.
E nding the fight is very hard.
N ow we are friends again.
D o you know how I felt?
S o it is a weird routine when I fall out.

Jessica Hardiman (8)
Henleaze Junior School

THE DOLPHIN

Darting through the water
It's gone in a flash
This dark blue figure
I think it's going to crash

Jumping out of water
This animal so swift
This dark blue figure
Is really rather fast

The figure's slowing down now
It's getting slower and slower
It's tiring out now
Suddenly it's stopped.

Laurie Churchill (10)
Henleaze Junior School

WHAT WILL THE MILLENNIUM HOLD?

What will the millennium hold?
Will all the writing be big and bold?
Will dogs still bark?
Will trees still hold bark?
Will we still be football mad?
Will the devil still be bad?
Will the candle still be made of wax?
Will sweets still come in packs?
Will we still be party animals?
Will there still be elephants and other mammals?
Will we still travel on planes?
Will there still be acid rain?

I wonder.

Aimi Mouser (9)
Henleaze Junior School

PIANO LESSON

Every Saturday I go to piano lessons.
Before piano lessons (which are at half past twelve)
I am worried,
I feel like the teacher there
Is going to tell me off for not doing it right.
Every Saturday I can't stop worrying,
But the good thing is,
It turns out just how I like it!

Caroline Roberts (8)
Henleaze Junior School

THE TURTLE

The turtle is a moderately slow creature.
It plods along on its fat four legs.

Its shell is as hard as rock
and if you tried to eat it, it would break your teeth.

The turtle is a sleepy creature as it plods
along at a moderately slow speed.

Ben Penny (9)
Henleaze Junior School

I LOOKED AT THE STARS

When I looked at the stars on the beach,
I felt very calm.
As the waves lapped along the shore,
The sand felt very warm.
As the water caught my toes,
I left that lovely land.

Molly Sherman (8)
Henleaze Junior School

A DAY WITH MY MUM

One day I was happy and gay,
It was not my birthday,
It was great fun.
That day it was a happy day,
I spent it with my mum.
That day I fed my fish,
I spent that day with my mum.
We went somewhere that day,
We bought chocolate
And played together
That happy, old day!
But then it had to end,
That happy old day,
I was very happy that day.

Lee Bennett (8)
Henleaze Junior School

THE DISOBEDIENT BOY

His work was neglected,
His appearance was scruffy and tatty.
But his house was picturesque,
Clean looking and grand.
Pity though.
The parents were fine,
And the boy so bad.
He comes home from school,
'Plonk' on the couch,
And there he stays for the rest of the day.

Jonathan Basker (10)
Henleaze Junior School

MY MUM

My mum is the best mum ever made,
She's special when she plays with me,
Reads to me in bed at night,
Hugs me tightly,
Or buys me sweets.
She's special when she tidies my room,
Plays on the Nintendo with me,
Buys me clothes,
Or says goodnight.
She's special when she remembers my birthday,
Cooks me meals,
Or sorts out my problems.
My mum pays for my holidays,
Puts up with me,
But she also cares for me (I hope).

Rebecca Rees (10)
Henleaze Junior School

CATS

They doze in the day and wail in the night,
They play with wool, they're full of spite.
Their keen, pointed claws, their soft, glossy fur,
Their malevolent miaow, their mellifluous purr.
They dine on fish like cod and plaice,
Their coned ears and triangular face.
Their padded feet, their glimmering eyes,
They get up early to watch the sun rise.
They like to chase birds, mice and rats,
I really love those critters, cats.

Eddie Notton (11)
Henleaze Junior School

FARM ANIMALS

Cows, horses, pigs and sheep standing at the gate
waiting for their friend, she's late.

As they watched the cars go by some of them to begin to cry,
'She'll never come now,'
They say as they watched some more cars go by.

As it gets dark they begin to say,
'She'll never come, she hasn't all day.'

Soon they got sleepy and went to bed.

As they were sleeping their friend came and she said,
'What a shame.'

She went away and muttered 'Another day.'

Charlotte Russell-Smith (8)
Henleaze Junior School

MATHS TEST

I am sitting in a maths test, we have got five minutes to go
I am on a sum I cannot do
Seconds are going quickly, now three minutes to go
I am raining sweat and grinding my teeth
I move onto the next sum and then do the rest
I go back to the sum I was stuck on
And then the maths' teacher says 'Time's up, hand in your paper'
I got it back yesterday and surprisingly I got an A.

Alexandra Neads (9)
Henleaze Junior School

MILLENNIUM

It's another 1000 years
Another time to say cheers
People will be partying very soon
Will earth design another moon?
Will Venus go to 0°c?
Will there be no bushes and trees?
Will the blazing hot sun die?
Will humans have three eyes?
Will we have gigantic flappers?
Will cats have blunt trappers?
Will we have electric cars?
Will we have people from Mars?
Will there be more dinosaurs?
Will there still be Santa Claus?
Will the blooming earth explode?
Thanks to our rubbish load
It's another 1000 years
Another time to say cheers.

David Browne (9)
Henleaze Junior School

FIRST DAY AT SCHOOL

My parents drive away leaving me outside.
A gigantic person exclaims my name.
They take us into a room.
We sing a little song.
Chips, beans and sausages, delicious.
Maths, English, science, whatever next!
What time's my mum coming Miss?
There out of nowhere, she comes into my mind.

Satvinder Dubb (11)
Henleaze Junior School

MY HOLIDAY

I went to Blackpool,
I felt so cool,
We had some sandwiches to eat,
With some cold meat.
I asked my mum for some sweets,
No! I'm reading on the seat,
We went home for tea,
I looked through the window and saw the waves in the sea.
We went to the park,
I heard a singing lark,
When I came home,
I was all alone.
It was nearly bedtime,
I heard some bells chime,
A star was shining I could see,
It was shining right on me.

Go to bed my mum said.

Stephanie Ting (9)
Red Maids' Junior School

THE SECRET OF ETERNAL YOUTH

Oh dear, oh dear, how can I find it,
Is there a scroll to unwind it?
Is it in field, bush or briar?
Is it left, right, lower or higher!
Oh dear, how can I find it?
I hope there isn't a scroll to unwind it,
I can't unwind a scroll you see,
Oh, why can't it just come to me!

Philippa Janssenswillen (8)
Red Maids' Junior School

THE FANTASTIC DAY

Whirlwind blowing,
Fire still glowing,
The stars are shining bright,
In the pitch black night.

It's a sunny morning,
And everyone is yawning,
We all smile in delight,
As we fly the colourful kite.

In we go for our tea,
While my mum is laying by the tree,
I said let's go to the ice-cream man,
Now I said, it's too hot, let's get the fan.

Back out we go in the sun,
When the night sky has just begun,
As the swings have just been swung,
Now it's the end of the fun.

Shannon Bryan (9)
Red Maids' Junior School

THE MILLENNIUM

There's five more seconds till the millennium,
Four, three, two, one, yes!
We're there - it's the year 2000.
There's banging and crashing outside,
The neighbours are having a party,
There's lots of noise, lots of fun,
It's the millennium, we're having a party,
I wonder what we'll do for the year 2001!

Abbey Chapman (10)
Red Maids' Junior School

THE WEEPING WILLOW TREE

The weeping willow tree,
Looks down at me,
With his bulging, big red eyes,
When the weeping willow tree
Looks down at me,
I feel sure that he spies.

Underneath the roots of the tree,
There is a hidden child,
And in the branches that I see,
I'm sure it's very wild.

Someday I'll go up to him,
And look underneath the roots,
With my hat, scarf and gloves,
And, of course, my wellington boots!

Rebecca Hutter (9)
Red Maids' Junior School

WITCHES

Round and round the witches go,
Some are quick and some are slow,
Dancing and prancing until it's dark,
Witches hate animals so watch out larks!

They stir their cauldron while it's bubbling,
If you walk past, you will be running,
That's all I know about terrible witches,
I'd better go,
There's one coming!

Hannah Petsounis (9)
Red Maids' Junior School

SATURDAY THE 20TH

Saturday the 20th of March is a very important day,
It's my auntie's wedding day,
My auntie has a braid,
I am the bridesmaid.

I have an embroidered shoe,
A silver horseshoe,
Denise is my auntie,
Deno is my uncle.

I am excited as can be,
There is a buffet for tea,
I really can't wait,
I'm frightened we will be late.

Lisa Marsh (9)
Red Maids' Junior School

ROUND AND ROUND THE GARDEN WE GO

Round and round the garden we go,
Through the rain and through the snow.
We will never know where we will go!
Less than treats there will have to be sweets.
Cobwebs lay but we still stay,
Lots of junk but still we jump.

Round and round the garden we go,
Through the rain and through the snow.
We will never know where we will go!
Lots of junk but we still jump,
Round and round and through the door,
Watch out for the muddy footprints on the floor.

Katie Iles (8)
Red Maids' Junior School

THE BOY IN THE STREET

The boy in the street
Could hear some feet,
Were they his or someone else's?
The quicker he bounds,
The louder they sound,
They flew on the ground,
They were witches,
They laughed and cackled.
They chanted a potion
That went like this,
Bat's legs, cat legs,
Frogs to spider's nose,
Tiger's toes, monkey's foes.
The boy ran home,
While he had the chance,
He woke up and he found,
He had been in a trance.

Alexandra Wilkinson (9)
Red Maids' Junior School

THE TRAVELLER

Upon a steamy, gloomy night,
A traveller came far from sight,
He travelled towards the castle blue,
Where he could see no-one but few,
The moon so tall stood upon the wall,
Gleaming in the night.

Lucy Brimble (9)
Red Maids' Junior School

MY HAMSTER

My hamster is called Lotty,
Lotty is not dotty,
Lotty is fast,
And has a strong grasp,
She has a soft nip,
And is bigger than a pip.

Lotty is fluffy and cute,
And could play the flute.
Lotty is five months old,
And doesn't get cold.
She has a good mood,
And likes her food.
I know she loves her ball,
And obeys me when I call.

Lucy Homer (9)
Red Maids' Junior School

THE PARTY

The antelope got up in the dark
Of the day, even before the lark,
He said I will pay
For a party today,
And invite Rachel and an ant called Mark.

But what if it rains or snows?
Or to a party that nobody goes?
We'll have alphabet soup
Which we'll drink from a hoop
As we dart and dance under rainbows.

Kirsty Wilkinson (9)
Red Maids' Junior School

THE MAGIC FLYING RECIPE

Mix and stir it,
Until it goes pop.
Add frogs and bat's legs,
Until it turns green.

> Boil it and stir it,
> Until it goes thick,
> Boil it and stir it,
> Add the blood of a witch,
> Until it turns pitch black.

Bake it and bake it,
Until it is hot,
Now it is ready,
Let's eat it and fly!

> It works really well,
> Why don't you try.

Emma Morgan (8)
Red Maids' Junior School

MY FAVOURITE PLACE

I have a favourite place at the bottom of the garden,
Where I sit all the time.
The tree is shady and in the summer I climb it.
It's fruity and a good place to hide.
It's my mango tree.
I have a favourite place, it's my mango tree.
It's, it's, it's, it's my favourite place.

Katharine Warbutton (8)
Red Maids' Junior School

THE SEA

I look at the sea,
When I'm up on the quay,
It reminds me of when I was three!
Just as happy and content as can be,
Feeling great, just to be me!

Mummy used to say, 'Look, there's a fish,
Quickly, quickly - make a wish!'
Then, that little fish would disappear,
With a little, teeny, tiny splish!

I look at the sea,
A big, big crash and then a splash!
I'm on the bay, a day in May,
Quietly here, peacefully I lay,
Lots of shells, thousands of yells.

I'll go for a paddle - ooh, lots of squeals!
Oh my lord - hope there's no eels!
'Excuse me sir, excuse me sir,
Are *you* going to answer *me*?'
'Are there *any* eels in here?
Oh for goodness sake,
I'll find out for myself!'

Ellen Crabtree (10)
Red Maids' Junior School

A LOONY BABOONY

A loony baboony
Lives on the moony,
And he's coming very soony,
In a spoony is that loony baboony.

Charlotte Lewis (9)
Red Maids' Junior School

THE SEA

The sea, the sea,
Oh! I long to be at sea.
The lapping waves, the tide and seashore.
The sea is always unpredictable,
One day, gently moving waves at your side,
The next, ripping waves, howling wind and pouring rain.
Anything which comes along is in the hands of death.
Fishermen go out in storms and risk their lives for us,
Collecting fish in their nets and bringing it back for us,
Collecting fish in their nets and bringing it back to port,
Then off they go again to do another round.
That's why I like the sea, and one day I'll be a heroic sailor,
Sailing all seas and searching every island,
Seeking my fortune.
Oh yes! That's the life for me.
The sea, the sea,
How I love the sea.

Rachel Colley (9)
Red Maids' Junior School

MY ROBOT

I love my robot,
He's my best friend.
Sometimes my friends can't play, but,
He's always there.

My mum loves him too,
Especially when it comes to ironing and cooking,
Sometimes things get burnt, but
He's always there.

My robot has a funny voice,
It's squeaky and jumpy,
But he's friendly and funny,
I don't know how he works, but
He's always there.

He follows me around on his wheels,
And loves it when I come home.
He sings me a lullaby and turns out my light.
Then I just dream,
And wish he was really there!

Emily Nolan (9)
Red Maids' Junior School

THE BARN OWL

A streak of white cuts the air,
A swoosh of feathers,
Sharp claws flash,
Soft flesh tears.

Chicks' hungry beaks turned skyward,
Mother returns from the hunt,
Squabbling and shrieking,
All wanting to be at the front.

Big orange eyes glint,
No escape for the prey.
Who would want to be a rabbit,
As night follows day.

Out from the barn,
The hungry mother flies,
The best hunter in Bristol,
With her big orange eyes.

Hannah Lipfriend (9)
Red Maids' Junior School

WITCH'S SPELL

Slowly glimpses of tinsel lightning in the air!
Slowly tumbling non-defeating wind,
A fist of rock pounding in the sea,
A dreaded death of joy,
Breathing out like God's almighty breath,
Millions of stones like hail with no defeating end,
Whirlwind of dust,
throwing of tide,
Swooping of tide,
Light mixed wind,
Non-failing wind, wind whistling madly,
Creaking, crackling and slashing fog like someone's black eye,
Sudden death and despair, clearing slowly, slowly, slowly.

Georgina Brooke (8)
Red Maids' Junior School

I HATE WRITING POEMS

I hate writing poems,
Particularly rhyming ones,
It's always difficult to find
A rhyme that rhymes with kind.
Hmm.
It's late at night,
My lips are tight,
There's too much light,
It's awfully bright,
Good night! Good night! Good night!
I've come to the end of the road,
Is that all right, Mrs Noad?

Sophie Clarke (9)
Red Maids' Junior School

THE OPTICIANS

When I go to the optician,
Someone looks in my eyes,
My mum tells them it hurts,
I think they tell a bunch of lies.
When I go to the optician,
Someone looks in my eyes,
I say it hurts *real* bad,
Then they believe my dad.
When I go to the optician,
Someone looks in my eyes,
I'm a brand new client,
I think they're *real* violent.
When I go to the optician,
Someone looks in my eyes,
But some of them just tell lies,
But then my illness dies.

Elizabeth Kitchin (10)
Red Maids' Junior School

WHEN GRANDAD FELL DOWN THE PLUGHOLE

When Grandad fell down the plughole,
He said *'Wip, wip, wip, woo!'*
He went down the pipes to the sea,
And then he lost his shoe!
He went up into the clouds,
And rained into the water tank,
He went down the pipes to the sink,
Feeling rather thirsty he said,
'I could really do with a drink!'

Natasha Colledge (9)
Red Maids' Junior School

SCHOOL DINNERS

Queuing up for dinner,
What's on the menu today?
Queuing up for dinner,
It's chips, *hip, hip hooray!*
Sitting down with dinner,
Dipping chips in sauce,
Sitting down with dinner,
I could eat a horse.
Finished with our dinner,
Now it's out to play,
Finished with our dinner,
Hip, hip, hip, hooray!

Anna Corrigan (10)
Red Maids' Junior School

MY OLD TREE

My old tree is knobbly and wobbly,
My old tree is as dark as a lark,
My old tree is not tall or small,
My old tree is wide enough to hide behind,
My old tree has twisty, misty roots.
My old tree has leaves of green and a slight lean,
My old tree,
My old tree, I will miss it when it's gone.

Nicola Johnson (10)
Red Maids' Junior School

MY HORSE

My horse is brown,
He is called Polo,
I can go fast on him,
But he is very strong,
I ride him up the road and back,
He is very good,
I love Polo lots and lots,
Especially when he is really, really good,
I could cuddle him all day,
I really, really could.

Egidia Wright (9)
Red Maids' Junior School

SOUNDS

I love the sound of my family, when I am snug in bed at night,
I hate the sound of someone when they've had a terrible fright,
I love (when I am not alone) the sound of peaceful silence,
I hate the sound, in every way, of certain, hateful, violence.
I love the sound of dinner, sizzling on a plate,
Except when mum cooks quiche, fish pie and apricot bake!

I love the sound, when in a brook, of water splashing *splish*,
I hate the sound of metal spoons, scraping on a dish.
I love to hear my teddies, purring in my bed, but I hate it when
My alarm comes on and starts echoing round my head!

Louise Glanvill (9)
Red Maids' Junior School

THE CAT, THE HAT AND THE MAT

The hat sat in the cat,
No!
The cat sat in the mat,
No!
The mat sat in the hat,
No!
I don't think I've got it right.

The cat sat on the floor,
No!
The floor sat on the hat,
No!
The mat sat on the cat,
No!
I don't think I've got it right.

The floor sat in the mat on the cat,
No!
The cat sat in the mat on the floor,
No!
The hat sat in the cat on the mat,
No!
I'll have one final try.

The cat sat in the hat on the mat,
Yes!
I think I finally did it.

Bethany Nutt (10)
Red Maids' Junior School

ROBOT WARS

When robots fall into the pit,
A very dark hole, no lights are lit,
The robot feels a lot of panic,
And remembers what happened to the Titanic.

They use the pick-axe to bash the other robots,
They fall apart and get all hot,
If the robots do get stuck,
They will need a bit of luck.

Instead of having a great sharp claw,
The robots have a big chainsaw,
Vicious teeth *whizz* round and round,
Making an awful crunching sound.

Tyrone McNama (8)
Romney Avenue Junior School

I LOVE BOOKS

When you read a book,
You can meet new faces,
And travel to different places.
You can fly in a balloon,
Or take a rocket to the moon,
When you read a book,
Lying down in your warm bed,
It can paint pictures in your head.
Some books are really funny,
They make me laugh until I hold my tummy.

Kye Simpson (8)
Romney Avenue Junior School

ARMY

The army is a powerful force,
They have to pass a special course.
Big green tanks roll along,
Sometimes soldiers sing a special song.

Tanks come in different shapes and sizes,
Captains and colonels the general advises.
Camouflage is green and brown or white and grey,
In the war if they get killed, there on the floor is where they lay.

Guns and cannons,
Big, loud noises,
Far too much,
For our small voices.

Danny Read (8)
Romney Avenue Junior School

SUMMER

Summer has come,
Everyone is playing.
Under the grass,
All the insects crawl around.
My friends play football every day.

My back garden is full of flowers,
Every day I go outside to sit in the shade.
Rhubarb grows,
And I pick it for my tea,
In the summer.

Luke Weston (10)
Romney Avenue Junior School

FOOTBALL POEM

Football is for me,
Unless you're a chimpanzee.
We can play football in all the cups,
Unless you're a pup.
Use your feet,
Unless they stink.
Get on the pitch,
Don't be a witch.

You can play in May!
4W win football, thanks to Danny Moore!
I will give him a round of applause!

Scott Bennett (9)
Romney Avenue Junior School

WHY DO WE HAVE TO LIVE?

Why do we have to live?
Life is so boring.
Why can't I be something else?
An animal will do.
Why do I have to be a human?
I'd love to be a great big whale.
'Oh God please change me.'
'I can't', says God,
'Why?' I say,
God says,
'You have to wait until you die.
'Why?'

Indarjeet Singh
Romney Avenue Junior School

BMX BIKING

My favourite hobbies are karate and
BMX-ing and playing on the PlayStation.
My most favourite of these is riding my BMX,
Because it is fun.
I like riding over the bumps and making the
Bike jump.
I like riding down the street to the shops,
I've just started trying bunny-hops.

Anil Saroe (8)
Romney Avenue Junior School

FOOTBALL

My favourite sport is football,
I always try to score,
But sometimes people push me on to the floor.
Sometimes I try to tackle,
But they go round me so I don't always get the ball,
Because they are so tall.

Jordan Campbell (9)
Romney Avenue Junior School

FOOTBALL

My favourite hobby is football.
I play it all the time at home,
I play it at school.
When it is 4W against 4H,
4W always wins.
Sometimes the score is 12-1 to us.

Jamie Owen (9)
Romney Avenue Junior School

ROMNEY AVENUE SCHOOL

School is great,
I won't be late,
Ten to nine, that's the time.
The bell goes *cling a ling ting ting*,
The whistle goes *toot*,
They're the signs to get in lines.
Go to class, just in time for maths.

At quarter past we leave the class,
To eat our morning break.
After that, literacy hour,
Guided reading for half an hour,
Some groups work in their English books.

Then it's service, time to sing.
Teachers read stories, especially Little Pete's,
They make the children laugh and giggle.

At twelve o'clock we go out to play,
Go down for dinner, *hip hip hooray!*
School dinners are very nice,
I like their hot curry and rice.

The desserts are even better,
Most of them have added sugar,
Then we go outside until one o'clock.
Then we come in and get on with some work.
Soon after that it's three o'clock,
Time to tidy up the class.
Then we go home to relax and rest,
Watch TV until half past eight,
Then get in the bath,
Then go to bed.
'Cos I promised my mum I won't stay up too late.

Natasha Sheppard (9)
Romney Avenue Junior School

WHY ARE WE HERE?

'Why are we here mum?'
'Please tell my why.'
'Why were we born?'
'I don't know why.'
'Please mum shout it out loud,
Or write it in a cloud.'
'Please mum tell me why.'
'I've got a headache,
Now shut your eyes,
And go to sleep.'

Princess Jackson (10)
Romney Avenue Junior School

FOOTBALL DAYS

Football is the best wherever we go,
Everyone is playing it.
Why should we waste our time by not playing it.
Everyone is cheering for our team,
Football is the best,
So don't waste your time!

Ashley Whale (9)
Romney Avenue Junior School

MY BEST FRIEND

My favourite friend is Laura,
She comes to me every time I call her.
She looked friendly when I saw her.
Yes, my friend is Laura!

Jade Davies (9)
Romney Avenue Junior School

Why?

Why do we die,
Why do we lie,
Why do we drink,
Why do we think?
We need to.

Why do we go to school,
Why do we play the fool,
Why do we play,
Why do we pay?
Well, I don't know.

Why do we laugh,
Why do we have a bath,
Why do boys wear pants,
Why do we dance,
Well, do you know?

Why do we talk,
Why do we walk?
Or maybe . . .

Chloe Smith
Romney Avenue Junior School

PLAYING

Playing is my best hobby.
I could play and play,
Really, all day.

I like playing with my friends,
The fun never ends,
Playing, playing, playing!

Laura Vile (8)
Romney Avenue Junior School

ANGER

Anger is like,
Hell on earth,
With red flames,
Licking the atmosphere.

Anger is like
A giant volcano,
Which could explode,
Whenever it wanted to.

It is a red devil,
As hot as a
Chilli pepper,
On a barbecue.

It is like,
An immense monster,
About to rent its rage,
On you.

David Harding (11)
St Augustine of Canterbury RC Primary School

AFRAID

My eyes stuck wide, irremovable glue holding them back.
My pupils get big, like a black hole in outer space.
Shaking so hard, like a washing machine out of control,
Won't move. I'm so still, with one hundred nails
Sticking me to the ground.
Not one joint in me will move . . . too afraid!

Victoria Kent (11)
St Augustine of Canterbury RC Primary School

STRESS

Stress is like a bee buzzing
Buzzing like a cooker
Sizzling like the toast

It is like your younger brother
Repeatedly asking you to play
Like the lady on the phone
When you've dialled the wrong number

It is like a raw wind
Wrapping around you
Like fire burning in your head

It is like a parrot squawking
Coloured as a rainbow
Flapping round your head

Stress is like a plague
Sweeping through the town
Quick! Before you catch it

Calm down, relax!
Breathe deeply in
Breathe deeply out.

Patrick Allinson (11)
St Augustine of Canterbury RC Primary School

THE FOGGY PAINTING

Fog, silent and still,
Like the gloomy grey background in a painting.
The talented artist,
Carefully smudging his different shades of grey.
Finally he finishes his beautiful work of art.

Roxanne Onuora (9)
St Augustine of Canterbury RC Primary School

WHAT IS FOG?

A witch's spell over the cauldron bubbling with smoke,
Frost spiralling, clouds coming down like grey air,
Creeping like a shadow under a thick cloak,
Floating while misting the glass windows in silence,
The ground freezing from the cold air,
Strange gases riding, skulking in every corner.

Emily Orlowski (9)
St Augustine of Canterbury RC Primary School

THE WIND

The wind is a rattlesnake,
Wildly rattling at steamed-up windows,
Hissing menacingly from the grey sky above,
Hardly spying his grey, camouflaged body.

Annalisa Hochstrasser-Jones (9)
St Augustine of Canterbury RC Primary School

SUN HAIKU

Boiling, red-hot waves,
Swirling like a million
Mad octopuses.

Isabelle Madams (10)
St Augustine of Canterbury RC Primary School

MOON TANKA

Moon, cold blue like thousands of
Manta rays in the deep sea.

Gillian Belton (11)
St Augustine of Canterbury RC Primary School

ANGER

Anger is fire burning,
A volcano erupting,
Lava pouring everywhere.

It is never-ending nails running,
Down a blackboard.
Boiling hot water spilt over you.
It's like a kettle screeching.

It's like the pits of hell,
Scorching your soul, being poked
By a red-hot poker.

Sam Price (11)
St Augustine of Canterbury RC Primary School

THE WIND IS LIKE A TARANTULA

The wind is like a tarantula,
Whisking and howling into the smallest gaps,
Banging windows, cracking doors,
Rattling shutters,
Searching for a soul to bite.
Venom still in the heart of this small, crawling beast.
Does it know that they're afraid,
Or does it think that it's a lonely place?
As it squeezes through a crack,
Will you realise that it's in your house?

Sam Allen (9)
St Augustine of Canterbury RC Primary School

THE WIND

The wind is a monkey,
Furry, brown,
Arms messing up tidy hair.
A naughty long tail,
Pulling you back,
He rattles window frames,
Banging wooden doors.
Scattering rubbish,
Without a care.

Emma Smardon (10)
St Augustine of Canterbury RC Primary School

AS BLUE AS A SPARKLING SEA

Blue is a sparkling sea,
Brighter than a diamond.
Blue is a gentle sky,
Covering every island.

Blue is a sneezing ice-cube,
Colder than snow.
Blue is on the English flag,
Which will never go!

Blue is the distant Pluto,
Softer than a bluebell that's free,
Smarter than a sailor's suit,
Going out to sea.

Light blue's mood,
Is gentle, quiet and calm.
Dark blue's mood,
Is wild and causes harm.

Joe Payne (9)
Sea Mills Junior School

184

AS RED AS A SUNSET

Red is a sunset in the sky,
Across which a million birds fly.
Red is a red, red rose,
As red as a cold nose.

Red is a heart beating fast,
Red as a sportsman running past.
Red is a crafty, cunning fox
Red as a baby with chickenpox.

Red is the colour of fire,
As it raises higher and higher.
Red is a poppy in its flower bed,
It is definitely my favourite red.

James Hutchinson (8)
Sea Mills Junior School

AS GREEN AS SOME DAZZLING GRASS

Green is some dazzling grass,
It's a massive evergreen tree,
Rustling leaves will always pass,
They lay on the ground like a sparkling sea.
Green is a croaking frog,
Splashing in the river,
A caterpillar on a log,
Going for a slither.
Green is a jumping cricket,
Green, I'll never leave it.

Ryan Williams (8)
Sea Mills Junior School

As Black As My Football Boots

Black is a deep, dark hole,
burrowing down like a mole.
Black is a sticky tarmac road,
steamrollers going past with their heavy load.

Black is bright,
but only on white.
Black is newpapers' print,
it can give you hints.

Black is extremely dark in space,
you cannot see an astronaut's face.
Black is a pitch black cave,
bats' wings fly past and wave.

Black is my football boots,
I score the winning goal when I shoot.
Black is the spooky night,
when stars twinkle bright.

Jordan Lovell (9)
Sea Mills Junior School

As Green As Grass

Green is some beautiful grass,
It's a gigantic green tree.
You will see lots of green in a great big sea.
Green is the largest football pitch,
The greatest I have ever seen.
Wellington Boots to hide in the grass
They can't see where you've been.

Derren Hann (9)
Sea Mills Junior School

As Orange As A Blazing Fire

Orange is a growling fox,
hunting out his prey.
Running round a tall old tree,
searching for his food each day.

Orange is a sparkly egg yolk,
sizzling in the pan.
If it is left there too long,
it will soon get a tan.

Orange is ginger hair,
swaying all around.
When the hairdresser cuts it,
it will then fall on the ground.

Orange is a new-made house,
standing on the street.
Orange is the blazing fire,
that always gives us heat.

Suki McFie (8)
Sea Mills Junior School

As Red As A Poppy

Red is like a bright red poppy,
In the wind it goes all floppy.

Red is like a burning fire,
Racing up, always higher.

Red is like a sunset in the sky,
Lots and lots of birds floating by.

Kita Davidson
Sea Mills Junior School

AS RED AS A BLAZING SUN

Red is like a red, red poppy,
blazing in the sun.
Red is a valentine rose,
sent with love to someone.

Red is a flaming sun,
burning in the sky.
Red is the colour of war,
soldiers marching by.

Red is the colour of blood,
running through your veins.
Red is the colour of dyed hair
and of Virgin aeroplanes.

Keon Baker (9)
Sea Mills Junior School

AS RED AS A RED, RED ROSE

Red as a blinding hot sun,
I like to have lots of fun.
Red is a frozen nose,
The colour of red, red rose.
Red is my banging heart
When I feel smart.

Red is a flaming fire,
I'm climbing higher and higher.
Red is for human blood,
Cooked by playing in mud.
Red is baubles on the Christmas tree,
With berries, crackers and everyone happy.

Gemma Poole (9)
Sea Mills Junior School

As Orange As A Pointy Carrot

What is orange? Orange is the sunset,
the sun sets in the sky.
What is orange? Orange is a blazing fire,
reaching up so high.

What is orange? Orange is a pointy carrot,
sitting in the ground.
What is orange? Orange is a dazzling egg yoke,
very squishy and round.

What is orange? Orange is some baked beans,
sitting in their tin all day.
What is orange? Orange is the blazing sunshine,
when we stay out too late to play.

Jenna Walsh (9)
Sea Mills Junior School

As Red As Strawberries

What is red?
Blood is red, flowing in your head.
What is red?
Poppies are red, lying in their flower bed.

What is red?
Strawberries are red, in the summer sun.
What is red?
A cold nose is red, in the snow having fun.

What is red?
Roses are red, you can smell them from ahead.
What is red?
The sun is red, spitting fire on your head.

Ruth Sterry (9)
Sea Mills Junior School

As Yellow As A Flaming Sun

Yellow is the flaming sun,
And we are having fun.
Yellow is a juicy melon,
And I have a juicy lemon.

Yellow is golden corn,
Swaying gently in the morn.
Yellow is gold sand,
Gradually sifting through my hand.

Yellow is high-lighted hair,
Eating a juicy pear.
Yellow is best coloured butter,
Butterfly, creamy moth, all a flutter.

Corinne Coombs (8)
Sea Mills Junior School

As Red As A Soft Velvet Hairband

Red is a flaming fire,
Flames leaping higher and higher.
Red is a cold, cold nose,
Cold right through, down to my toes.

Red is on the Russian flag,
And on my favourite school bag.
My pencil case at home is red,
I keep it underneath my bed.

Red is a soft, velvet hairband,
Red is snapping crabs in the sand.
Red is a beating heart,
Red is a big jam tart.

Hayley Weeks (9)
Sea Mills Junior School

As Blue As A Watery Sea

Blue is a bright diamond
Which lays on an island,
Blue is a big bubble,
Floating around without any trouble.

Blue is a watery sea,
Floating around free.
Blue is a freezing ice,
Marking items lower price.
Blue is a bright sky,
Wide, far and oh so high.

William Russell (9)
Sea Mills Junior School

As Red As A Bullseye

Red is a bright bullseye,
Glaring up at the sky.

Red is your heart beating,
Or your cheeks, on being caught cheating.

Red is a bright, bright, rose,
Tickling my little toes.

Red is my beautiful crimson hairband,
Which I hang gently on my jewellery stand.

Jodie McMeechan (8)
Sea Mills Junior School

EAGLE

Golden Eagle flies and swoops
Powerful hunter fiercely shines
Sharp-eyed creature now attacks
Beautiful bird flying by.

Jamie Hodgkins (8)
Sea Mills Junior School

THE EAGLE

Eagle flying through the sky
Golden, bright swooping down.
Nesting up in mountains high
Gliding over fields and towns.

Luke Long, Cara Farrell, Elizabeth Kimber
Christopher Price, Luke Johnstone
Sea Mills Junior School

FLAMINGO

Beautiful flamingo floating by
Colourful creature in the sky.
Wearing stilts, no longer flies
Slowly walking with head held high.

Craig Down (9)
Sea Mills Junior School

AS RED AS DANGER

Red is a sign of danger,
It's an angry, bright sun.
Running around like an animal,
Children laughing, having fun.

Red is the colour of anger,
To make a bull get cross.
Red for the best known roses,
To soften the sadness of loss.

Donna Smith (9)
Sea Mills Junior School

FLAMINGO

Beautiful creature floating by
Slowly walks with head held high.
Pink flamingo, legs like stilts
No longer reaching for the sky.

Curtis Littler (8)
Sea Mills Junior School

TURTLE

Turtle slowly creeping
Under his shell so lonely.
Gently paddling in the sea,
Will you come along with me.

Danielle Heavens
Sea Mills Junior School

HORSE

Excited creature trotting along.
Jumping, playing and running alone.
As he gallops through the field.
Suddenly stops to eat his hay.

Holly Elson (9)
Sea Mills Junior School

RED IS A BLAZING HOT SUN

Red is a blazing hot sun,
When we're all having fun.
Red is a red, red rose,
A lovely smell up my nose.
Red is a fire engine speeding along.
The red car is too long.
Red is blood going all the time
When the sun shines.
Red is a man running past.

Daniel Brown (9)
Sea Mills Junior School

TIGER

Tiger fiercely walks
As he slowly stalks
Powerful animal running by
Eyes so bright light up the sky.

Mitchell Leigh (9)
Sea Mills Junior School

MOUSE

Running, swooping, passing silently by.
Creeping upon his spongy paws.
Small friendly mouse squeaks soundlessly,
Stops and looks around with a pause.

Ben Doyle (8)
Sea Mills Junior School

CAT

Furry cat
Creeping by
Stalks his prey
Then runs away.

Tasha Harvey (9)
Sea Mills Junior School

SPIDER

There was a spider from China
he's going to be miner.
He saw a snake
and hit it with a rake.
And now he's a climber.

Thomas Thurston (9)
Sefton Park Junior School

THE SNAIL

The snail is a slimy thing.
It has no legs or wings.
It crawls around
upon the ground
and is a hideous thing.

Florence Greenland-Hall (10)
Sefton Park Junior School

MY DREAM

I would put in my dream:
The tail of a twisting shooting star.
A sunset burning on the ocean.

I would put in my dream:
A bee buzzing on the end of a buttercup.
A dragonfly whizzing through the air.
A seagull screeching through the sky.
A sun burning on the hot sand.

I would put in my dream:
Indians fighting with guns.
Cowboys fighting with bows and arrows.
Sand slithering through our hands.
Water splashing and little specs of colour flying.

Lee Mitchell (10)
Sefton Park Junior School

SOLDIER

I drive a tank and an air-strike plane.
I carry a pistol and a rifle.
I wear combats and throw grenades.

I make tents and tie up ropes and
I load up all the guns.
Despite all the fun, I still miss my mum.

Although I protected a million people
I'm glad I'm home with my mum.

Nyame Stranger (9)
Sefton Park Junior School

I WALKED ON THE SHORE

I walked on the shore.
I had nothing better to do.

The waves of the sea
were higher than me.

As the days passed
the water grew fast.

The cliffs were high
as skyscrapers.

When I swam in the sea.
It was as relaxed as me.

Joseph Johnstone (10)
Sefton Park Junior School

THE RED PLANET MARS

I wish I was on Mars.
Up there amongst the stars.
Exploring volcanoes, canyons
and caves, trying to find
something strange.

I dream about flying a
shuttle all the way to Saturn.
To skate on the rings from dawn to night
then I'll come back tomorrow.
I want to live on Mars.
Up there amongst the stars.
And jump around and have all day.
I want to live on Mars!

William Nixon
Sefton Park Junior School

MY FAMILY ACROSTIC

M eal cooker
U mbrella buyer
M y mum.

D oes gardening
A car fixer
D rinks beer.

S weet eaters
I s kind
S creams a lot
T ea throwers
E ats a lot
R ed hair
S weet and cute.

C uddly
A miaower
T ammy's her name.

B enjamin is his name
R eads - not!
O nly one
T ooth grower
H eadache maker
E arly riser
R eal talker.

F ishy smells
I love my fish
S melly water
H e is Jonathan and she is Gemma.

M enace is me
E asy believer.

Rachael Milner-Lunt (9)
Sefton Park Junior School

MY FAVOURITE MONKEY

I like little monkeys.
My favourite is a chimp.
They're black on their body
they're white on their head.
They're pink on their face
and they are the cutest
animal I have ever seen.

Ashley Barnes (10)
Sefton Park Junior School

ANIMALS

I like animals I hope they like me,
they are furry and soft
and as cute as can be.
Some are big, some are small.
Some are wide, some are tall.
Some are horrible, some are nice.
Some are scared of things like mice.

Karl-Johan Gasiorek (10)
Sefton Park Junior School

THE CORNER

Every day - all day long.
I sit in the corner, where I belong
but if one day I'm very good
I sit at the table and eat my
cooked food.

Samantha Coggins (10)
Sefton Park Junior School

WALKING TO SCHOOL IN THE RAIN

Walking to school in the rain
wondering if I'll get the cane.
Splish, splash, splosh
now my shoes aren't so posh.
My sweater is soggy
so is my doggy.
Socks, shirt - all wet.
How wet can it get?
Now the journey slowly ends
so I can see my soggy friends.
As I enter the classroom
there are shallow puddles on the floor.
Out in the hall I see more.
Sally is singing a soggy song
to get rid of the muddy pong!

Katerina Lockett (10)
Sefton Park Junior School

IN MY WORLD

In my world the flower within the bud burning the sun.
The purest water from the purest river
runs into the sea.
There is no salt in the sea.
Salt comes from a special type of rush
there are plenty of trees no war or disease.
You have to believe to get into my world
you've got to believe before you see.

Samuel Varcoe (9)
Sefton Park Junior School

That Boy!

That boy sitting next to me.
He is as cute as can be.
I gave him a card
but he saw me and said
'Next time you do that, you'll be dead!'
So I don't like that boy anymore.
I love the boy sitting opposite me.
Well he gave me a card so sweet and kind
but I still think that boy sitting next to me
is as cute as can be.
That boy in the other class
he's as weak as a piece of grass.
But on Valentine's Day . . .
Well I can't tell you it's private!
I think I'll stay away from *boys* now.

April Pearson (10)
Sefton Park Junior School

The Magic Flame

My flame's ashes are full of magical things.
The magic of a mountain nymph.
The flash of a dragon's scales.
And the flow of the running river.

The power of a hurricane.
The ire of lightning.
And the might of a whirlpool.

A book from an apprentice.
A spell from a magician.
And a wand from a sorcerer.

Stefan Williams (10)
Sefton Park Junior School

I HATE GREENS

Cabbages, cauliflower, sprouts and beans
have one common name and this is *greens*.

Beans and spinach, broccoli and sprouts
should all be thrown out.

I hate the lot!
Cabbages, cauliflower - especially peas.

My mum always says 'Eat your *greens*!'
But I never do.
So I'll give them to you!

I would never eat them - not for a million pounds.
Well maybe one day, just for fun.
I'll eat them for my mum.

Leanne Roost (10)
Summerhill Junior School

GUESS WHO?

I'm yellow and tubby
Soft and cute.
Red's my colour, honey's my food.
Guess who? Guess who?
Yes! You guessed . . .
It's Winnie the Pooh.

Amy Conaboy (9)
Summerhill Junior School

FOOTBALL FEVER

I play football every week
at the local college we all meet.
We are all girls in our team
to win matches is our dream.

Our Coach always trains us hard.
We've never had any red or yellow cards.
I usually end up being in goal
I hope I don't miss any of the balls.

Practising, training, saving shots.
Boy oh boy! Do we get hot?
One day I hope that we'll succeed
in being top of our football league.

Kerri Edgar (8)
Summerhill Junior School

MILLENNIUM COUNTDOWN

Only one year to go, hip, hip hooray.
The year 2000 is coming soon.
The world will turn a new face
and so will we.

People pray for peace and health.
1, 2, 3, 4 the Millennium countdown.
5, 6, 7, 8 we will take another step into the future.
Children's cheers at midnight on the first day when the hour chimes.
Celebrations, praise will be held on the last strike of the clock.
1, 2, 3, 4 the Millennium countdown.
5, 6, 7, 8 we will take another step into the future.

Chloe Allward (10)
Summerhill Junior School

THERE WAS A DOG

There once was a dog
who loved to go for a walk, a run, a play.
Whenever her ball did she see
she runs to the door
with a bark, bark, bark.
Waiting for her lead to be put on,
then to the park did she go.
For a roll and tumble and play.
When it was time
home did she come
for a chew and a drink.
And when it was time
for a short sleepy sleep
she heard a funny bleep.
So she went back to sleep
and she got on her feet.

Jenny Frampton (9)
Summerhill Junior School

MY DOG HARVEY

My little dog sleeps all day
he never ever wants to play.
He doesn't like going out at night
because the dark gives him a fright.
He has got lots of hairs
he's not allowed to climb up the stairs.
Sometimes Harvey catches fleas
that jump around and like to tease.

Samuel Bracey (9)
Summerhill Junior School

THE WILLOW AND OAK

You are a sad widow
weeping of your loss.
You are shielded by your leaves
and you have your privacy.
You are the least thought of
you pray for your loved one to come back.
You curve to drink from the cool river to
quench your thirst.
You're low down to the oak - a big bully.
He's fat and muscular and he stands with pride.
He looks down like a king
and looks at the smaller creations
of the other trees.

Oliver Holt (10)
The Meadows Primary School

THE WEEPING WILLOW

You are a weeper
who shows only yourself what you hold
under your wondrous leaves.
You are a widow who's lost all but yourself
in all that you have.
You're soft and gentle as you call to nature.
And now still - you hang as still as the night
and when day comes you hang as none.
But all is not lost if you stand up for your loss
and now you are there loving and caring.
Holding up your leaves so all can see
your wondrous leaves.

Stephanie Crosse (11)
The Meadows Primary School

WILLOW WHY DO YOU WEEP?

Oh willow! Why do you droop?
And why do you weep?
Is it because of the young you lost
long ago?

Yes! It is the oak.
I am getting old, I cannot cope.
I cannot cope with the great old oak.

I am his servant, as are my friends.
We serve him with air and water
for him we fend.
He is so big, we are so small,
at us he bawls.
We are annoyed.
We are angry.
We still serve him
but for how much longer?

Thomas Cole (11)
The Meadows Primary School

THE GREAT OAK

Oh mighty oak - you are a king.
So big, so tall, so grand.
Your branches reach up to the sky.
You are known for miles around.

Your long thick trunk.
Your dark green leaves.
Your branches sway in the sky.
Under the glow of the moon.

Hannah Webb (10)
The Meadows Primary School

SNOW

You are as cold as the Antarctic.
You are as white as a polar bear.
You are as cold as an iceberg
living in the deep.
You cover the land like a blanket
of fur as soft cotton.
You are the snow queen of weather.
You are the maker of hypnotism
to make children come out and play
in your rich cloak of fur.
You're a child's fantasy.
You make children smile.
You're snowflakes are a diamond necklace.
You are as white as a dove.
As clean as new fresh rain.
You are as soft as clouds
and when the sun comes out you go
and come back again next year.

Holly Bryan (11)
The Meadows Primary School

WEEPING WILLOW

A cold sleeper with protective hair.
Weeping all night long.
A sad old lady with nowhere to go.
She whistles on her way to heaven.
Her hair is soft and gentle as it sways in the wind.
But you can still hear her weep.
Whether it be night or day.

Daniel Watkins (11)
The Meadows Primary School

SHE THE WEEPER - THE WILLOW

The willow is old and wise
she gives advice in her old ways.
With soft weeping hair she protects others;
whilst she prays for youth once more.

Every night she cries, and why?
Ask the grandmother of all, being wise,
for she protects young saplings
for she knows all the answers.

She whispers kind chants,
and makes a shelter for all.
A child's hideout for years
she slowly closes her gentle eyes once more.

A thousand whispers she has spoken,
a million spells she has chanted.
For she is the life protector of all;
and she is an old-weeper by the stream.
Who can see people's secrets in her reflection.

She worries all day, everyday and never stops to rest.
But waits for the day when she can see her loved one again.
Her days have been long and the same.
She, the lonely pessimist;
closes her eyes for the last time
and sleeps forever with sweet memories
of her past life.

Sara Grady (11)
The Meadows Primary School

WILLOW

You are an old lady widow.
As your tired eyes rest on your pillows
you weep in the park all night
as your hair glows in the moonlight.

Your long branches flow
through the wind as it blows.
As your long hair bends into the river
your body starts to shiver.

As we speak now
the old willow hangs its bough.
Resting peaceful in the earth.
As we remember the old willow's birth.

Calley Williams (11)
The Meadows Primary School

THE WEEPING WILLOW V THE POWERFUL OAK

Old lady willow
why are you so sad and lonely?
An old grandma, soft, gentle, life-protector.
Weeping widow why do your branches hang so low?
Are you praying to your loved one who died long, long, ago?

You are strong, big and muscular.
You are the king of all trees.
Long-living, powerful and thick.
You are tree - over power.
Mighty, young and foolish.

Lauren Davies (10)
The Meadows Primary School

OLD LADY WILLOW

You spend your life sweeping
the ground beneath you.
Holding secrets inside.
You think of the grave,
That makes you a widow
who weeps on the dusty ground.

Your branches fall down
and you pray all your life.
You are soft and gentle and wise.
You like to be lonely, protective and sad
and are frail the rest of your life.

You quietly whisper
to God in the wind.
And keep your old head bowed.
You're in the dark patch of the earth.
His hand is where you lay,
slowly, sadly you pass away and collapse
in the hell of the grave-land bay.

Clare Pearce (11)
The Meadows Primary School

THE OLD WILLOW

The old weeping widow
cries to the gods of the trees.
As she protects her loved ones
with her long rusty hair.
She's old, tired and wise,
but she still stays alive
with her walking stick by her side.

Max Holder (10)
The Meadows Primary School

THE PESSIMIST AND THE OPTIMIST

I - the pessimist - the weeping widow
bows down praying to my lost loved one.
My long hair swaying across the ground.

A protector of all around
my children long gone.
A lonely grandma waiting, crouching,
whistling for my days to be gone.
I - the pessimist willow.

I - the optimist,
the king of the trees,
the light of life.
Willows from all around bow down
praising me, the rest cowering away.

I - the powerful one
stand strong on my trunk.
Tree - overpower.
I - the optimist oak.

Charlotte Timmis (10)
The Meadows Primary School

THE GREAT OAK

Your trunk is thick, your branches wide.
You stand above all, mighty and high.
You make fun of others younger than you.
Tall, great and powerful, by and by.
The tall great king of the trees you are.
Long-living, mighty but foolish.
Your descendants are spread afar.
They and others look up at you in respect.

Julia Tilley (11)
The Meadows Primary School

WHISPERS

The willow by the water
reaches down to quench her thirst
from her day of protecting
her secret beneath the earth.

But her friend living sad in a lane.
Weeps for the loss of her loved one.
No children to care for - not any.
Not wanting her life to go on.

The oak tree big, tall and muscular
laughs at the sad, weeping trees
and teases them night and day.
For the oak tree can do as he pleases.

The willow takes no notice
her heart is too broken to care.
For the oak is just a child
and his tricks are easy to bear.

Francesca Roberts (11)
The Meadows Primary School

THE OLD WEEPING WILLOW

The willow bends over
the grass and the clover.
Praying to the one
that she lost in October.

Her hair hangs down
to the grass on the mound.
She makes never a move
and never a sound.

Rachael Freestone (11)
The Meadows Primary School

THE WILLOW

The willow, so soft and sad.
You stand alone, weeping, weeping.
The life-protector of them all,
so wise and gentle, sleeping, sleeping.

So quiet, slow and still.
Soft, wise words you are saying, saying.
The silent night comes creeping in
to hear your spirits, praying, praying.

The darkness stays, it's never ending.
The wind moves branches, swaying, swaying.
Your branches see the day awakening.
Dawn breaks and the sun is staying, staying.

Your saplings break through the ground below.
You can hear the leaves ringing, ringing.
The trees stand tall, bending, protecting the ground.
This is what the spring is bringing, bringing.

Michelle Osborne (11)
The Meadows Primary School

THE WILLOW TREE

The weeping willow breaks down in tears
as she looks for traces of her long-lost loved one;
Protecting something with her droopy arms,
but what? We shall never know.

Your gentle long hair covers your gnarled old face.
You're the wisest tree that ever could have grown.
You're like an old grandma sitting with her knitting
waiting for the day when all lies peacefully.

Richard Howes (10)
The Meadows Primary School

WILLOW

W would you think that I am a widow?
I pray for my lost mate.
L lonely am I and forever will be
L lost and alone
O on my own I cry
W with tears as cold as ice.

Laura Gratton (11)
The Meadows Primary School

WILLOW

Oh willow! Why are you so sad?
Your long hair hangs down so low.
You are very protective
of your loved one.
You are old and wise.

Laura Friend (11)
The Meadows Primary School

THE STRONG OAK

Your branches are like iron bars.
Your trunk is as strong as steel.
The king of trees is your name,
searching for the perfect dame.
The others all bow down to you
they do whatever you want them to.

William Wagstaffe (11)
The Meadows Primary School

THE OAK AND THE WILLOW

You stick your big roots in the ground
Keeping you up through rain and storm.
Your bark protects your chunky trunk
For 24 hours each day.
Your Muscular branches growing so long
Towering over everyone just like King-Kong.

You are the king of trees
The mighty worshipped one.
The grass bows down before you
Worshipping you the mighty one.

And then there's the feeble willow tree
Standing sad in the dark corner of earth.
Your hair covers the whole of your body
Right from your head to your toe.

You come nowhere near the importance of the
Mighty great oak tree.
You don't deserve to be a tree
But a blade of grass.

Robert Purnell (11)
The Meadows Primary School

THE OLD WILLOW VERSUS THE OAK

Old widow grandma bends down praying
to the mighty oak.
The oak stands proud - full of power.
Whilst the willow is casting a shadow
of sadness in the early night.

Michael Herring (10)
The Meadows Primary School

A SNOWY DAY

I woke up one morning
it was snowing a lot.
I put on my coat and hat
'cause it's not very hot.

I go outside
it's very white.
I get a snowball
and throw it out of sight.

I go inside
and have a quick dinner.
I go out again
the snow's getting thinner.

I look around
'Here comes Tom.'
The sun comes out
the snow's all gone.

I go inside
and have a bath.
I'm already dreaming
of the snowy path.

Lucy Rodrigues (10)
The Tynings Primary School

DAVE THE DRAGON

High in the mountains,
deep in a cave.
Lived a little red dragon
with the name of Dave.

Fire from his nostrils
burnt out the whole lake.
Burnt out all the fishes.
Burnt out all the snakes.

His long scaly tail
swishes in the air.
He has some sharp white teeth,
and a purple tuft of hair!

He dines on meat and human feet.
He really is so bad.
A terrible little dragon.
A very naughty lad.

Tom Tainton (10)
The Tynings Primary School

RUBBISH

R educe your rubbish
U se as much of your rubbish as possible
B ins are useful on the street to put rubbish in which has been dropped.
B ins are around in the street - *so use them!*
I n Bristol there is lots of pollution
S ome families fill five black sacks a week.
H omes waste at least 50% of what could be used again.

Patrick Wood (9)
The Tynings Primary School

CELEBRATION 2000

Out with war
In with peace
Out with hunger
In with food for everyone
Out with diseases
In with health
Out with racism
In with equality.

No more bad feelings
Lots more happiness
No more bullying
Lots more understanding
No more anger
Lots more joy
No more loneliness
Lots more friendship
No more hate
Lots more love.

Karl Taylor Hopkins (10)
The Tynings Primary School

THE MOON, THE EARTH

Here I am sat at my window
gazing up at the earth.
Such a wonderful planet,
I wonder why humans left it
It looks so beautiful, peaceful and different.

Luckily I'm going on holiday there tomorrow
me and my family.
I can't wait to just go off somewhere
and sit under a tree.
Just sit there and think and think all day long,
maybe until I'm grey and old.

Isabel Crew (11)
Wick Primary School

PARTIES ARE THE TIME TO . . .

Parties are the time to celebrate.
To chill out with your best mate
and stay out to 2 o'clock
so you can't see the front door lock.
At a party all you eat is junk food,
to wake up in a really hyper mood.
And stay in bed till midday
because that's the perfect way to
stay.

All the parties in time to come.
Maybe in the next millennium.
Will they party like we do today?
And stay in bed all day.
At parties will they only eat junk
food?
Because that's perfect, to stay in the
mood.

Ashley Longman (10)
Wick Primary School

LIFE IN THE NEXT MILLENNIUM

What will it be like?
Floating cars and motorbikes.
Trains that work up in the sky,
you get on low and go up high.

Shopping will be done by TV and by phone,
your goods will be brought direct to your home.
No more queues to wait in, no hours with aching legs.
No more dropping shopping bags to splatter all your eggs.

No farms will exist, no pigs eating swill,
no pork chops for us, just a vitamin pill.
No cows in the fields, no sheep on the hills.
We'll swallow our tablets and chew on our pills.

Our skies may be different, our days may be long.
The climate is changing, our seasons all wrong.
Shorts in the winter and trousers in spring,
jumpers in summer, what a silly thing.

But things might be different and turn out quite nice.
As long as we're happy, we will pay the price.
Look after the world, all creatures and plants.
We may have some beautiful
non-biting ants!

Naomi Iles (9)
Wick Primary School

STREET CHILD

As I sat in the street today,
I watched the people go this and that way.
I watch the people try to catch the train,
or only just get on the bus again.

I could hear the subway roaring below,
This was a place where no river would flow.
No grass would blow in the cool morning air,
I feel the dust in my hair.

I hugged my blanket tight and warm,
and watched a person's car.
I thought of those with comforting homes,
I was not one of them by far.

I remember my mother leaving me on the step,
but everyone rejected me.
I grew up feeling cold and wet,
knowing that I must flee.

I was only two when she left me,
so very far away.
On that cold, wet and dark night,
I could only wait for the day.

For I watch the people go this and that way,
I'm being flung away each day.
I need somebody to always say,
I'll never ever send you away.

Alice Dixon (10)
Wick Primary School